American History
READER'S THEATER
DEVELOP READING FLUENCY AND TEXT COMPREHENSION SKILLS

Written and Edited by
Alaska Hults

For Dr. Bonnie Milne Gardner

Illustrator: Corbin Hillam
Cover Illustrator: Amy Vangsgard
Designer: Jane Wong-Saunders
Cover Designer: Barbara Peterson
Art Director: Tom Cochrane
Project Director: Carolea Williams

Table of Contents

 = total number of parts

INTRODUCTION

Fluency instruction provides a bridge between being able to "read" a text and being able to understand it. Readers who decode word by word sound plodding and choppy. They are too busy figuring out the words to think about what they are reading. Fluent readers are accurate, quick, and able to read with expression. They make the reading sound interesting. Beyond the experience of the listener, fluent readers are also demonstrating skills that are crucial to their understanding of what they read. Fluent readers recognize words at a glance, group words into meaningful phrases, and move beyond the struggle to decode individual words. They are able to focus on making sense of what they read.

Reader's Theater is an exciting way to help students improve reading fluency without being too time intensive for the teacher. It requires no props and no additional teaching skills on your part, and it is not difficult to manage. Reader's Theater promotes better reading comprehension because students who have learned to read a passage expressively also come to better understand its meaning. In addition, research says that these gains transfer well to new text. Reader's Theater also addresses standards in listening while providing a fun environment for everyone involved. When students practice their lines, they read and reread the same passages. Under your direction, they gradually add more expression, read more smoothly, and find any subtle meanings in the passages.

The scripts in *American History Reader's Theater* are intended to be read in large groups of 6 to 13 students. Each script is prefaced by an activity that focuses on vocabulary from the script, the factual and fictional background of the piece, fluency instruction specific to that script, and comprehension questions that span the levels of Bloom's Taxonomy. Each script is followed by one or two whole-class activities related to the content of the script. These scripts are designed for fluency instruction. While they are based on factual information about the time period or characters, many of the characters and scenes are entirely fictional. The overall purpose is to provide students with text at their reading level that is fun to read. The background section that precedes each script provides additional information about the characters or the period around which the script is built. All the scripts provide the following hallmarks of a good Reader's Theater text:

- fast-moving dialogue
- action
- humor
- narrative parts

American History Reader's Theater provides hours of fluency practice that is grounded in the familiar format of American history with characters students know and may even admire. The large-group format gives students an opportunity to work together to craft an entertaining reading for a peer or adult audience.

HOW TO USE THIS BOOK

Each Reader's Theater script should be covered over the course of five practice days (although those days do not need to be consecutive). The first day should include some or all of the elements of the suggested reading instruction. It should also include an expressive reading by you of the script as students read along silently. On each of the following days, give students an opportunity to practice their reading. On the final day, have each group read its script for the class.

Five sections that support reading instruction precede each script. You will find **vocabulary, background information** for the script, a **brief description of each character,** specific **coaching for fluency instruction,** and **comprehension questions** that progress from the simplest level of understanding to the most complex.

On the first day of instruction, briefly discuss with students the vocabulary. Each vocabulary list includes a short activity to help students understand the meaning of each vocabulary word. For example, the vocabulary activity for The Age of Exploration (page 7) asks volunteers to pantomime the meaning of each word.

Next, use the background and information about each character to tell students what the script will be about and describe the characters.

Read aloud the script, modeling clear enunciation and a storyteller's voice. Do not be afraid to exaggerate your expression—it will hold the attention of your audience and stick more firmly in their minds when they attempt to mimic you later. Model the pacing you expect from them as they read.

Finish the reading instruction by discussing the fluency tips with students and having them answer the questions in the comprehension section.

Now it is time to give students a copy of the script! Use the following schedule of student practice for a five-day instruction period.

Day 1	After following the steps outlined on page 4, give each student a personal copy of the script. Pair students and have Partner A read all the parts on the first page, Partner B read all the parts on the second page, and so on.
Days 2 and 3	Assign students to a group. Give each group a script for each student, and have each student highlight a different part. Have students gather to read aloud the script as many times as time permits. Have them change roles with each reading by exchanging the highlighted scripts. Move from group to group, providing feedback and additional modeling as needed. At the *end* of day 3, assign roles or have students agree on a role to own.

Day 4	Have each group read aloud the script. Move from group to group and provide feedback. Have students discuss their favorite lines at the end of each reading and why the manner in which they are read works well. Repeat.
Day 5	Have each group perform its script for the rest of the class (or other audience members provided by buddy classes and/or school personnel).

Throughout the week, or as time permits, provide students with the activity or activities that follow each script. These are optional and do not have to be completed to provide fluency instruction; however, many provide students with additional background information that may help them better understand the characters or setting of the script.

Additional Tips

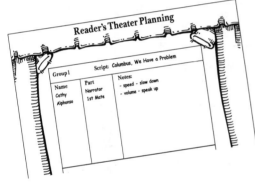

- Use the Reader's Theater Planning reproducible (page 6) to track the assigned roles for each group and to jot down any informal observations you make for assessment. Use these observations to drive future fluency instruction.

- Notice that there are no staging directions in the scripts. These plays are written to be read expressively in a storyteller's voice. If the focus is placed on *acting out* the script, students will shift their focus from the reading to the movement. If students become enchanted with a script and want to act it out, invite them to do so after they have mastered the reading. Then, have the group go through the script and brainstorm their own staging directions (e.g., page 54: *Ruth slaps Billy playfully on the arm*) to jot in the margins.

- To fit fluency instruction into an already full day of instruction, it will work best to have all groups work on the same script. This will permit you to complete the first day's activities as a whole class. Students will enjoy hearing how another child reads the same lines, and some mild competition to read expressively will only foster additional effort.

- If you have too many roles for the number of students in a group, assign one child more than one part.

- If you have too many students for parts, divide up the narrator parts. As a rule, these parts tend to have longer lines.

- The roles with the greatest and least number of words to read are noted in the teacher pages. The ⬆ and ⬇ indicate a higher or lower *word count*. They are not a reflection of reading level. The narrator parts usually reflect the highest reading level. However, less fluent readers may benefit from having fewer words to master. More advanced readers may benefit from the challenge of the greater word count.

Reader's Theater Planning

Group 1	Script: _____	
Name	**Part**	**Notes:**

Group 2	Script: _____	
Name	**Part**	**Notes:**

Group 3	Script: _____	
Name	**Part**	**Notes:**

American History Reader's Theater © 2004 Creative Teaching Press

THE
Age of
Exploration

AMERICAN
HISTORY

VOCABULARY

Discuss each of the following words with students. Then, have volunteers pantomime the meaning of each word in some way. (Students can point to the East Indies on a map.)

animatedly: in a lively manner

crow's nest: a place for a lookout to stand at the top of a mast so as to be able to see further along the horizon

destination: intended end of trip

East Indies: the western European name, during this period, for Eastern Asia

first mate: the second most important officer on a ship

suitable: right for a purpose

BACKGROUND

It is early morning and only a handful of the boat's crew are awake. Land was sighted the night before, shortly after midnight. On the captain's deck stand the captain, the first mate, and the navigator. They disagree over whether they have come to the place they are seeking—the East Indies. This script includes the following facts: land was sighted shortly after midnight, some members of the exploring party suspected almost immediately that they were not in the East Indies, Columbus never did believe that he had found an entirely new land mass, and it was the sight of the gold worn by the first natives that he met that motivated the other sailors to stay.

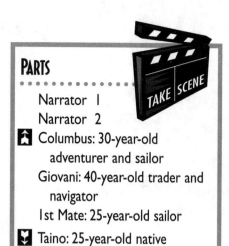

PARTS

Narrator 1

Narrator 2

Columbus: 30-year-old
  adventurer and sailor

Giovani: 40-year-old trader and
  navigator

1st Mate: 25-year-old sailor

Taino: 25-year-old native

FLUENCY INSTRUCTION

Have students discuss the ages of the characters to help them reflect the maturity level in their reading. When you read aloud the script for students, have them listen for the following:

• The pace of the reading speeds up when a character is excited. Have students name at least three places where the reading pace will pick up in this script.

• The pace slows down when someone is angry but trying to be polite. Have students name two characters who are angry but polite at some point in the story.

• Your tone of voice is always respectful of the other two characters when you speak for the first mate.

• Your voice rises at the end of a question, such as on the line
  Columbus: *Exactly how far?*

COMPREHENSION

After you read aloud the script, ask students these questions:

1. What is the name of the navigator?

2. Which character would you most like to play? Why?

3. How does Giovani figure out this land is probably not the East Indies?

4. Why do you think Columbus disagrees with him?

5. Why do you think that the discovery of gold convinced the sailors to stay?

COLUMBUS, WE HAVE A PROBLEM

PARTS

Narrator 1
Narrator 2
Columbus: 30-year-old
   adventurer and sailor
Giovani: 40-year-old trader and
   navigator
1st Mate: 25-year-old sailor
Taino: 25-year-old native

Narrator 1: It is early morning and only a handful of the boat's crew are awake. The entire ship was up celebrating most of the night after the man in the crow's nest cried "Land ho!" shortly after midnight.

Narrator 2: On the Captain's deck stands an old trader and navigator of average size and a large, muscular man the crew calls First Mate. They are talking in low voices with an older man who holds a map. The man with the map is waving animatedly as he talks.

Giovani: The sky is wrong for the East Indies.

Columbus: Well, clearly, the map is wrong.

Giovani: No, sir. I drew it myself when I visited her coast as a young man.

Columbus: Perhaps the sky has changed!

Giovani: And with it, the land? Sir, I do not know how to tell you this, but this is not the East.

Columbus: I think you are wrong.

Giovani: It does not look at all like this, sir. It would not have changed this much in the ten years I have been gone.

Columbus: Perhaps it is some outer island. You would have sailed from the other direction! Perhaps you did not make it this far east.

Giovani: With an entirely different sky? We are still very, very far from our destination, sir.

Columbus: Exactly how far?

Giovani: See those stars on the horizon, sir?

Columbus: Yes, I see them.

American History Reader's Theater © 2004 Creative Teaching Press

COLUMBUS, WE HAVE A PROBLEM

Giovani: They should be more or less behind us.

[There is a moment of complete silence.]

Columbus: I have always had a lot of respect for you, Giovani. You know that.

Giovani: Yes.

Columbus: So you know I do not mean to insult you when I say I think you are wrong.

Giovani: Yes, I feel the same way.

Columbus: You feel what way?

Giovani: That I have much respect for you even though you are, in this case, wrong.

Columbus: I spent more than 15 years researching this trip, Giovani.

Giovani: I know you worked very hard to get to this place, sir.

Columbus: I have spoken with some of the most learned men of our time.

Giovani: You have lots of support from some very great men, sir.

Columbus: Surely the Queen and King would never have permitted me to come if they did not feel sure that I knew what I was doing.

Giovani: Actually, I think they just thought they did not have much to lose now that the primary trade route to the Indies has been closed. If we do make it, they will soon be rich.

Columbus: And WE shall be rich. I know we are not far! I can feel it! I can almost smell the spices on the air!

1st Mate: [sniffing] I do not think those are spices you are smelling. Someone just emptied the chamber pots.

Columbus: It was just a saying . . .

Giovani: But you admit some of those great men disagreed with you.

Columbus: They thought the Earth was bigger than I do.

Giovani: Perhaps it is! Perhaps we are only, about, oh, halfway there!

Columbus: I am not wrong! China is only on the other side of these islands!

Giovani: What if it is not?

American History Reader's Theater © 2004 Creative Teaching Press

COLUMBUS, WE HAVE A PROBLEM

Columbus: I will not discuss that! There is no sense talking about the ridiculous. How could there be an entire mass of land still undiscovered in these modern times?

1st Mate: [coughs] It does not really matter as long as we can discover spices or new foods or…

All: Gold!

1st Mate: Well, then, let us hope there are great riches here so the men do not mind that we are lost.

Columbus: We are not lost! Giovani cannot remember his own mother's birthday. How can he remember the sky over China from ten years ago? This is probably an island south of Japan. We will do some trading here and then sail north a bit to find Japan.

1st Mate: And from there China?

Columbus: Yes, from there China!

Giovani: You are being incredibly stubborn!

1st Mate: I wish I knew which of you was right!

Columbus: Look, they told us it would take up to a year to arrive in the Indies. I have led you safely here in only 36 days!

Giovani: We did make excellent time to wherever we are.

Columbus: We have plenty of food and supplies left. We will take a few men ashore tomorrow and find some of the local people.

1st Mate: Maybe they can tell us where we are!

Giovani: If we can understand them. There are many, many different languages in the Indies.

Columbus: And many islands! You both are worried over nothing. I believe our fortunes are assured.

1st Mate: What are your instructions for today?

Columbus: We will look for a good spot to land and pick a crew to go ashore. Judging from the sky, we will have excellent weather for the next few days.

Narrator 1: The crew find a suitable place to anchor and a small party of men head to shore in a smaller boat.

Narrator 2: They carry with them some swords, some small items for trade, and two flags to represent Spain. Curious islanders cautiously come out of their hiding places to greet the visitors.

American History Reader's Theater © 2004 Creative Teaching Press

COLUMBUS, WE HAVE A PROBLEM

Narrator 1: It soon becomes clear that the natives have never seen metal weapons like the ones the Spaniards are carrying.

1st Mate: Be careful!

Taino: Ouch!

1st Mate: Those are called swords. They are very, very sharp!

Columbus: Hey, look at that!

1st Mate: His shirt? It is a nice shirt!

Taino: Want to trade?

1st Mate: Sure! My shirt for your shirt?

Taino: When was the last time you washed your shirt? No, I want that cloth you are carrying instead.

1st Mate: Hmmm, nope. It is a flag. I need to stick it in the ground to claim this island for Queen Isabella.

Taino: For whom?

1st Mate: We can talk about that later. How about this rope?

Taino: Hmmm, strong, nicely wound, might be good for fishing. OK, my shirt for your rope.

1st Mate: Great!

Columbus: Ask him for his nose ring!

1st Mate: Oh, no. I do not believe in nose piercing.

Columbus: It is not to wear! I want to see if it is gold!

1st Mate: Ooooh! Hey, friend. How about this red cap for your nose thing?

Taino: Sure! Nice hat! Thanks!

Narrator 1: The island inhabitants wear gold jewelry in their ears and nose and around their neck and arms. The desired spices that Spain is searching for are nowhere to be seen, but there is strong evidence of an even greater resource.

Narrator 2: The explorers, motivated to continue by the sight of gold, are now eager to stay and learn more about the islands they have found.

American History Reader's Theater © 2004 Creative Teaching Press

RELATED LESSONS

The East Indies

OBJECTIVE
Illustrate and describe the importance of the East Indies to western Europe in the mid-1400s.

ACTIVITY
In advance, gather **research materials** about 15th century Europe, Africa, and Asia. Display a **world map.** Explain that the reason that people of western Europe, including the countries of England, Spain, France, and Portugal, wanted to find the East Indies was because it was a source of a very profitable trade for spices. Previous to this time in history, the trade routes were over land. However, religious and political wars had closed key cities on the way to the East Indies over land. The first country that could find a way to the East Indies over water could become very rich. Give each student a sheet of **drawing paper** and access to the research materials. Have the class generate a list of questions they have about the area and the time period. Then, have students find more information about the East Indies (southeastern Asia and its islands) in the 15th century to answer the questions. Ask each student to write on drawing paper a paragraph that answers one of the questions and illustrate it. Bind the papers together in a class book entitled *15th Century Southeast Asia.*

Columbus, the Man

OBJECTIVE

Learn more about Christopher Columbus and his life.

ACTIVITY

Divide the class into pairs of students, and give each pair a **1' x 3' (30.5 cm x 1 m) strip of butcher paper, a meter stick,** and **research books** such as an encyclopedia or children's magazine articles about Christopher Columbus. Give each pair a **Christopher Columbus reproducible (page 15),** and have students research his life to complete the reproducible. Then, have students use the reproducible to create on the butcher paper a time line that shows the major events of his life. Have students use the space above or below the dates to illustrate each event. To extend the lesson, invite students who finish early to add additional dates for events in his life that are not on the reproducible but for which they discovered information in their research.

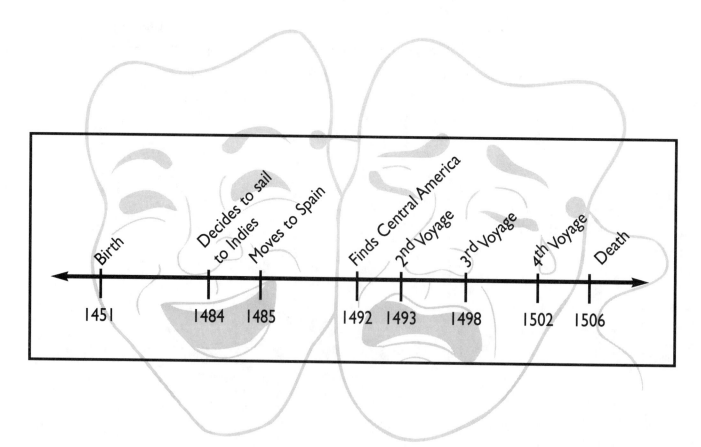

Names_____ Date _____

Christopher Columbus

Directions: Find the date for each of the following events in the life of Christopher Columbus. Then, on a long strip of paper, create an illustrated time line that shows each of these events.

Event	Date
Christopher Columbus' birth	
First decides to sail to the East Indies. Tries to convince King John of Portugal to back his plan	
Moves to Spain	
Sails for the East Indies and discovers Central America	
Sails for America the second time	
Sails for America the third time	
Sails for America the fourth time	
Christopher Columbus' death	

THE CARIBBEAN, 1700

AMERICAN HISTORY

VOCABULARY

Discuss each of the following words with students. Then, have students choose one word to define and illustrate.

cask: a large wooden barrel that carried necessary supplies, especially food and drink

plantation: a very large farm

quarters: private living space; usually reserved for the captain and one or two of his officers

smallpox: a very serious, often deadly disease

stow away: to hide on a ship without paying for or earning passage

watch: the period of time that each division of crew either is on deck (on duty) or below deck (at ease)

BACKGROUND

A boy and girl stow away on a trading ship bound for Spain. They are discovered and must face the captain. Elements of life at the time that are reflected in the script include the cargo of rum, sugar, and tobacco. A ship of this kind would have had an entirely male crew. The men would sleep on boards on the casks to optimize the storage space for the cargo. Only the captain had any real rights, and he was the sole voice of authority on the ship. Rats were a problem. They ate the supplies and spread disease. The route is accurate for the time and there would have been a stop in Cuba for tobacco. The trip home is not mentioned. Depending on the maturity of your students, you may wish to discuss with them that by this time, most of these crops were planted, cared for, and harvested by slaves from Africa. The ships that carried agricultural goods back to Europe would return later in the year with human cargo from the coast of Africa.

PARTS

Narrator 1
Narrator 2
Captain: 45-year-old man
Francisco: 1st Mate
Man 1: crew member
Man 2: crew member
Maria: 8-year-old girl
Raul: 9-year-old boy

FLUENCY INSTRUCTION

Have students discuss the ages of the characters to help them reflect the maturity level in their reading. When you read aloud the script for students, have them listen for the following:

• The volume of the reading increases when a character is in a large, open space or calling across a distance. Have students name at least one place where the reading volume will increase in this script.

• Enunciating words very slowly and clearly is another way to show anger. Have students name at least one place where a character might speak this way.

• The volume decreases when someone is hiding, speaking in a small space, or having a conversation he or she does not want overheard. Have students name at least one place where characters would talk more quietly. Model a "stage whisper" for students. Point out that the characters cannot really whisper or the audience will not hear them.

• Your voice rises very steeply at the end of a question that is both an exclamation and a question, such as when Man 1 says *I think this rat is a girl?!?*

COMPREHENSION

After you read aloud the script, ask students these questions:

1. Who was the captain?

2. How would you describe Francisco?

3. If you had been the captain, how would you have reacted to the news that there were two young stowaways on the ship?

4. Why do you think the captain was so concerned about the children?

5. Do you think this could really have happened? Why or why not?

STOWAWAY!

PARTS

Narrator 1
Narrator 2
Captain: 45-year-old man
Francisco: 1st Mate
Man 1: crew member
Man 2: crew member
Maria: 8-year-old girl
Raul: 9-year-old boy

Narrator 1: It is mid-afternoon and a warm breeze blows across the Caribbean Sea.

Narrator 2: The year is 1700 and a small ship with a crew of 20 men is sailing off the coast of Central America.

Captain: Turn the watch!

Narrator 1: The captain signals the crew to change. The men sleep on wooden boards that are placed on top of the food casks. There isn't enough room for everyone, so half the crew sleeps while the other half works.

Narrator 2: It has been a busy week, but the crew just loaded up on provisions and is heading to Cuba to pick up a load of tobacco. From there, they will head to Spain.

Captain: I have a funny feeling about this run, Francisco.

Francisco: How so, Captain? Loading went smoothly. We are full of good rum and sugar and expect to load up on tobacco at the next stop. The silver we carry is hidden in your quarters. Things seem to be going as well as can be expected.

Captain: I don't have any particular reason. I just feel funny about things. I cannot quite put my finger on it.

Francisco: Maybe there is odd weather on its way.

Captain: Maybe so. Go check on the men, Francisco. Then get some sleep yourself.

Francisco: Aye, aye, Captain.

Narrator 1: The first mate heads below deck to check on the men.

Narrator 2: There seems to be a commotion in the back.

Francisco: Is there a problem, men?

Man 1: I think we got a rat, Francisco!

American History Reader's Theater © 2004 Creative Teaching Press

STOWAWAY!

Francisco:	Ten years at sea and this is your first rat?
Narrator 1:	There is laughter from a dark corner.
Man 2:	Not that kind of rat! This rat has, let's see, teeny tiny ears …
Man 1:	No tail! Although this rat does have a little pink nose!
Maria:	Ow! That's my nose!
Raul:	Hey! Don't pull so hard!
Man 2:	C'mon, rats! Come into the light where we can see you!
Francisco:	Oh, no! How did this happen?
Man 1:	Hey! I think this rat is a girl?!?
Maria:	I am not a rat! What is the matter with you?
Man 1:	With me? Hey, I am not the one who thought it was wise to stow away on Captain Menendez's ship!
Francisco:	I cannot imagine there was much thought put into this at all. What are you kids doing on this ship?
Raul:	We tried to sign on. We were willing to work!
Francisco:	You are far too young.
Maria:	We aren't too young to starve to death though!
Raul:	We lived at the big sugar plantation.
Francisco:	Which one?
Raul:	The one by the peninsula.
Francisco:	Go on.
Raul:	My father was a tutor to the owner's sons.
Man 1:	So you are accustomed to, what, a few chores? How will you get by here when it is nothing but eat, sleep, and work?
Man 2:	And not very much eating.
Raul:	You have to let us stay. When the smallpox swept through it took our parents. The owner would only let us stay if we worked in the fields.

American History Reader's Theater © 2004 Creative Teaching Press

STOWAWAY!

Francisco: I don't mean to be unkind, boy, but that work might have been easier.

Maria: I can read, sir. I can write. Surely I can help the captain with his work somehow!

Francisco: He will have to answer that. What is your name?

Maria: I am Maria. This is my brother, Raul.

Francisco: I am taking you to the captain. You had better hope he is in a good mood. He can have you thrown overboard, you know.

Raul: Yes, sir. Thank you, sir.

Narrator 2:   The first mate takes the children above deck.

Captain: Francisco, tell me two of my crew ate something very bad and they shrunk.

Francisco: I do not think so, Captain.

Captain: Then tell me I ate something bad and I am seeing things that aren't really in front of me.

Francisco: I see them, too, Captain.

Captain: Speak up, kids. I am about to become extremely angry.

Raul: Captain, sir, I am Raul and this is my sister, Maria.

Maria: We want to work, Captain! It was never our intention to ride for free!

Captain: I believe, children, that we already have a full crew! And what on earth did you think you could do? This is no place for children!

Maria: Well, sir . . .

Captain: I am not done talking! What safe place can I find you to sleep? What healthy food can I feed you?

Narrator 1:   The children are silent and look unhappily at their feet. The silence stretches into a few minutes.

Captain: I am not going to feed you to the sharks.

Raul and Maria: Oh, thank you, Captain!

Captain: But absolutely no one rides on my ship for free!

Raul and Maria: No, sir, Captain!

American History Reader's Theater © 2004 Creative Teaching Press

STOWAWAY!

Captain: And you are only going as far as Cuba.

Maria: Sir, we had really hoped to sail with you to Europe! We think we might still have family there in Madrid.

Captain: What family?

Raul: Our aunt lives near the cathedral.

Captain: Really? I have a cousin in that area. Who is your aunt?

Maria: Regina de la Vasquez.

Captain: Does she have eight children?

Maria: Yes, sir. All boys. All older than Raul and me.

Captain: You must be Alfredo's children!

Maria: Yes! Yes, Alfredo was our father!

Captain: Well, that changes everything! Francisco, put Maria and Raul in my quarters. I cannot have my young cousins living with those rough men below.

Francisco: Yes, sir!

Captain: But I will not have you be lazy either. Maria, you will maintain my ship's log and keep the quarters of myself and the first and second mate absolutely spotless.

Maria: Yes, sir!

Captain: Raul, you will be my errand boy and help the cook with meals. Francisco, let the cook know I found him an extra pair of hands.

Francisco: Aye, aye, Captain.

Captain: You will work very, very hard on this voyage, and you will promise me that when we get to Spain you will seek out your aunt and never, ever go to sea again.

Raul: Yes, Captain. We promise. We are very grateful, sir.

Maria: I promise with all my heart, Captain.

Captain: All right. Now, all three of you need to get to sleep. We will be at port in a few hours and there will be work to do.

Francisco, Raul, and Maria: Aye, aye, Captain!

American History Reader's Theater © 2004 Creative Teaching Press

Central America Now

OBJECTIVES

Examine a map of Central America. Identify the countries, identify common map elements, and use the key to answer questions.

ACTIVITY

Write the questions shown below on **an overhead transparency,** and display it. Copy the **Central America Now reproducible (page 23)** onto an overhead transparency, and copy a class set. Give each student a reproducible. Have students copy the questions onto **lined paper.** Have them follow the directions for coloring the map at the top of their reproducible. (This will give them time to familiarize themselves with the map.) Then, read aloud the directions, and display the map transparency. Discuss with the class the questions and how each one can be answered. Then, divide the class into pairs, and have them use the map to answer the questions together on the lined paper.

QUESTIONS

What does the compass rose tell the map reader?
What does a star represent on this map?
Which country is found south of Nicaragua and northwest of Panama?

CLASS MAP DIRECTIONS

Find and circle the words that identify the North Pacific Ocean.
Draw a box around the compass rose.
Underline the word that identifies the island in the northeast corner of the map.
Draw a smiley face next to the capital of Costa Rica.

Name_____   Date _____

Central America Now

Directions: Use crayons to color each country of Central America as it is today. Then, fill in the key to show which color represents each area.

Key

Mexico = ☐   Guatemala = ☐   Belize = ☐

El Salvador = ☐   Honduras = ☐   Nicaragua = ☐

Costa Rica = ☐   Panama = ☐   ▬ = political boundary

Jamaica = ☐   ★ = capital city   — = river

NANTUCKET, 1720

AMERICAN HISTORY

VOCABULARY

Discuss each of the following words with students. Then, have them find each word in the dictionary, copy the definition, and write the guide words from the dictionary page for that word.

ambergris: a waxy substance found in the digestive tract of a whale

baleen: a part of the mouth some whales have instead of teeth

errand: a short trip taken to perform a specified task, usually for another person

mutiny: a rebellion on a ship

responsibilities: duties or obligations

scallywag: a mischievous person

schooner: a sailing ship with two or three large sails

scoundrel: a villain or rogue

sibling: a brother or sister

BACKGROUND

In the early 1700s, Nantucket was the center of the American whaling industry. In this story, the characters are loosely drawn from the youth of Benjamin Franklin. There really was a whaling ship called the *Dolphin* at this time and it was registered to a native of Nantucket Island. By that time, the onboard try-works had been invented and the route described by George Bunker is accurate for whaling ships of that period. They were gone about 6 months at a time, then came home to unload, clean, and make repairs for about a month. The parts of the whale that were most valuable were the ambergris, the blubber which was melted into oil, and the baleen from the whale's mouth.

PARTS

- Narrator 1
- Narrator 2
- *Grandpa
- *Captain: Captain of the whaling ship, first cousin to the kids
- George: 1st Mate on the *Dolphin*
- James: 11-year-old boy
- Mary: 9-year-old girl
- Sarah: 9-year-old girl
- *Ben: 8-year-old boy

One student can read these three roles.

FLUENCY INSTRUCTION

Have students discuss the ages of the characters to help them reflect the maturity level in their reading. When you read aloud the script for students, have them listen for the following:

- The pace of the reading speeds up when the children are excited. Have students name at least three places where the reading pace will pick up in this script.
- Your voice pauses at a comma. Reread the line
  Mary: I don't know, but I do not want to look anymore.
  Have students identify other lines that contain a comma and practice reading those with an exaggerated pause.

COMPREHENSION

After you read aloud the script, ask students these questions:

1. Where does the story take place?
2. Describe what you know of the whaling ship.
3. Which part would you choose to read in this story? Why?
4. What do you think the advantages are to an oil that does not smoke?
5. How do you think spending part of his childhood on this island might have influenced Benjamin Franklin as he grew older?

THE SCHOONER

PARTS

Narrator 1
Narrator 2
Grandpa
Captain: Captain of the whaling
    ship, first cousin to the kids
George: 1st Mate on the *Dolphin*
James: 11-year-old boy
Mary: 9-year-old girl
Sarah: 9-year-old girl
Ben: 8-year-old boy

Narrator 1: It is mid-morning and a cool breeze blows across Nantucket Island.

Narrator 2: A small group of children is gathered around a pond in the backyard of a large, white house. Each child has a tiny new frog to release to the pond.

Sarah: Oh, it really is soft! Look how small it is! There it goes! Bye, frog!

Narrator 1: They hear a voice calling from a distance.

Grandpa: Children!

All Kids: Here!

Grandpa: Where is Ben? I need him to run an errand for me.

James: We'll find him, Grandpa!

Grandpa: Thank you, James. Tell him I will be in my study when you find him.

Narrator 2: James, Mary, and Sarah run off to find their youngest brother. They check his favorite places such as the seashore and the library of their grandfather's house.

Narrator 1: But he is nowhere to be found.

James: He left without milking the cows again!

Mary: He said he would help me hang out the quilts to air this morning and then he disappeared!

Sarah: He did not fill the firewood rack!

James: I do not think he did any of the things he was supposed to do this morning. When I find him, I am going to talk some sense into him! He may be the youngest boy, but he still has some responsibilities!

American History Reader's Theater © 2004 Creative Teaching Press

THE SCHOONER

Narrator 2: For all of their searching, they were unable to find Ben.

Sarah: Where could he be?

Mary: I don't know, but I do not want to look anymore. I saw Captain Coffin down by the dock and he invited me to look around on the ship this afternoon.

Sarah: Captain Coffin said they spent all last week cleaning it out! Wait a minute! The ship! What if he went down there this morning?

James: That has to be it. Probably Captain Coffin invited him on the ship, too!

Narrator 1: The children ran over to the docks. There, they found their cousin, Captain Peter Coffin.

Narrator 2: Captain Coffin headed a large schooner that traveled for up to six months of the year hunting sperm whales.

Captain: I see the whole gang is here!

Sarah: Did you see Ben this morning, cousin?

Captain: Aye, he was looking around the docks and I thought he might get in the way, so I told him he could explore on the deck of the *Dolphin* as long as he avoided the crew.

Mary: He ran off this morning without finishing his chores!

James: I had to milk his cows.

Sarah: We need to find him.

James: He can do some of our chores this afternoon!

Captain: It is a regular mutiny you have going here! Well, I will not interfere, but I am too busy to help you find the scoundrel. The first mate is George Bunker, and you can ask him if he knows where the scallywag got to.

James: Thanks, Captain.

Narrator 1: The children board the *Dolphin.* Immediately, they are approached by a very large man. He looks fierce.

Narrator 2: Sarah hides behind James.

George: Ho! Don't be afraid of me little one. But do tell me what brings you to the ship!

James: We are looking for Ben. He has some chores to finish up.

THE SCHOONER

George: I have not seen him in a few hours! Is he still on the boat?

Sarah: We think he may be.

George: Well, then, let's look about!

Mary: James says you have the biggest schooner in all of Nantucket!

George: No, I would not say that, but she is a fine boat. She has two masts and two onboard try-works.

Sarah: Try-works?

Mary: They boil the blubber of the whales the crew catches in the pots on board.

George: It means we can stay out longer and hunt more before coming home. When I was younger, we had to bring the whales back here to the island before we could slaughter them. Now we use these big pots.

James: Have a look inside! Maybe he climbed in!

George: If he did, he will regret it. They are hard to get completely clean.

Sarah: No, he's not in there.

Mary: Mother says you were gone six months this time.

George: That's right. We went to Africa and back in that time.

Sarah: Do you catch right whales, sir?

George: If we see them, Sarah, but we have come to prefer the sperm whales.

Sarah: Mother says the oil is better in the lantern.

James: It does not smoke as badly as the other whale oil.

George: And sometimes you find a treasure in their stomachs.

James: Gold?

George: Ambergris.

Mary: What is ambergris?

George: It is a soft, yellow wax. You add it to fine perfumes to make them last longer.

James: Oh, well, that can't be worth much then.

American History Reader's Theater © 2004 Creative Teaching Press

THE SCHOONER

George: Just because you have no use for it, does not mean someone else does not, James. Ambergris is worth as much as gold. This is your cousin's cabin.

Mary: Where is the whale blubber?

James: It is stored below.

George: Right, we take what we need from the whales we catch and dispose of the rest. The blubber is melted and put in large barrels.

Mary: Can we see?

George: They were unloaded as soon as we came to port last week. It's empty down there now. Next week or so, we will load up again with empty barrels for the trip north for the summer.

Sarah: How empty? Could a child hide down there?

George: He might. It is kind of dark though.

James: May we go look?

George: Sure. The way down is along that ladder. Be very careful, kids. The ladder is steep.

Narrator 1: The children take turns going down the steep ladder. At the bottom, they must pause to let their eyes adjust to the dim light. The ceiling is low and the room is very large and very empty.

Narrator 2: But an odd sound rises and falls softly in the room.

James: Do you have a dog? I hear heavy breathing.

Mary: There he is!

Sarah: Wake up, lazy bones! You have work to do!

Ben: What? Why are you all here?

James: We will give you the list of reasons on our way back!

Mary: First, Grandfather wants to see you!

Sarah: Then, we need to see you.

Ben: For what?

Everyone Else: For WORK!

Narrators: The group heads back up the ladder, arguing back and forth, in the direction of home.

American History Reader's Theater © 2004 Creative Teaching Press

RELATED LESSON

Read and Respond

OBJECTIVE
Identify the purposes and consequences of early American whaling.

ACTIVITY

Give each student an **American Whaling reproducible (page 31)** and a **Thar She Blows! reproducible (page 32)**. Review the questions on the Thar She Blows! reproducible so students know what to listen for as you read. Read aloud the American Whaling reproducible, and have students follow along on their copy. Then, divide the class into pairs, and have each pair answer the questions on the Thar She Blows! reproducible. Discuss the answers as a class.

ANSWERS

1. Blubber, bones, and baleen were valuable to the colonists.
2. Before boats were used to hunt whales, the colonists waited until they washed up on shore.
3. Schooners would be gone about six months on a hunt.
4. The whales went to water around Iceland for the summer.
5. Whaling ships could eventually stay out for up to two years.
6. No, most large whales are still endangered.
7. It was dangerous to hunt whales with a handheld harpoon.

American Whaling

Directions: Read the information and then answer the questions on the Thar She Blows! page.

When the colonists came to America, they harvested beached whales for blubber, bones, and baleen. As time passed, they began to catch whales to make money. A person would watch for whales from shore. When a whale was seen, the person would sound the alarm, and men would jump in boats and row out to spear the whale with handheld harpoons.

By the early 1700s, bigger, faster ships could go further out into the ocean to hunt whales. New inventions allowed sailors to melt the blubber into oil that could be stored in barrels in the hold. For the first time, the whalers did not have to bring each whale they caught back to shore before they could catch another. They sailed their ships south across the equator, then east to Africa, north to Europe, and west home again. They would unload the whale products, clean and repair the ship, and then follow the whales north to Iceland for the summer. These trips would last up to six months. Later, American whaling ships could stay out at sea up to two years.

For most of history, men in small boats killed whales with handheld harpoons. There was no danger of extinction with such limited technology. Today, we do not hunt whales, because as technology improved, too many whales were killed. Most large whales are still very scarce.

American History Reader's Theater © 2004 Creative Teaching Press

Thar She Blows!

Directions: Read the questions. Use the information on the American Whaling page to answer each question in a complete sentence.

1. What parts of the whale were valuable to the colonists?

2. Before boats were used, how did the colonists harvest whale parts?

3. Schooners were sometimes used in the early 1700s to hunt whales. About how long would they be gone on a hunt?

4. Where did the whales go during the summer?

5. What was the longest amount of time that a whaling ship would stay out?

6. Have the whales completely recovered from overhunting during the early 1900s?

7. Do you think it was safe or dangerous to hunt whales with a handheld harpoon? Why or why not?

American History Reader's Theater © 2004 Creative Teaching Press

THE FIRST
SCHOOL FOR
THE DEAF IN
AMERICA

AMERICAN
HISTORY

VOCABULARY

Discuss each of the following words with students. Then, have students discuss why these words might be important to understanding the script.

expansion: the increase of a country's size by the acquisition of new territory

glance: to look at briefly

honorable: held in high esteem

spies: sees

triumphantly: proudly

willingly: doing something without being forced

BACKGROUND

Thomas Gallaudet is home visiting his parents when he notices a neighbor girl who is not playing with the other children. His brother explains that the child cannot hear. Gallaudet decides to try to communicate with her and, in the process, establishes a bond that will lead eventually to the first school for the deaf and the birth of the sign system that will become American Sign Language. This scene between Thomas Gallaudet, Teddy, Alice, and Mr. Cogswell is believed to have happened more or less as it is described here, until the final page. The decision to try to found a school happened over the course of the days following the first lesson between Thomas and Alice. The other characters are fictional.

PARTS

⬆ Narrator 1

Narrator 2

Narrator 3: narrates for Alice,
   a deaf child

Thomas Gallaudet: young man
   visiting his parents

Teddy: 12-year-old brother

⬇ Edward: 10-year-old brother

Emily: Alice's 12-year-old sister

Mr. Cogswell: Alice's father

FLUENCY INSTRUCTION

Have students discuss the ages of the characters to help them reflect the maturity level in their reading. When you read aloud the script for students, have them listen for the following:

• Thomas slows his speech somewhat when he is talking directly to Alice. It does not help her understand him, but it is instinctive for people to slow their speech when they know they are talking to someone who does not easily understand them.

• As a group, the children speak more quickly than the two adults.

• Your pace picks up and your pitch is higher when you read the lines for Mr. Cogswell after Alice writes her own name. You are anxious to see her educated and excited that you may have finally found her a teacher who can help.

COMPREHENSION

After you read aloud the script, ask students these questions:

1. Where does the story take place?

2. What is the difference between Alice and the other children?

3. How could you change your voice to show how excited Mr. Cogswell was by the end?

4. How would you have tried to communicate with someone who could not understand your language?

5. Why do you think Thomas Gallaudet was successful at starting his school?

THOMAS AND ALICE

PARTS
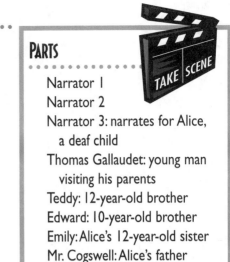

Narrator 1
Narrator 2
Narrator 3: narrates for Alice, a deaf child
Thomas Gallaudet: young man visiting his parents
Teddy: 12-year-old brother
Edward: 10-year-old brother
Emily: Alice's 12-year-old sister
Mr. Cogswell: Alice's father

Narrator 1: It is early June at a home in Connecticut. The United States is only 30 years old and there are only 17 states in the Union.

Narrator 2: It is a time of vast growth and opportunity for early U.S. citizens. Families tend to be large.

Narrator 1: Honorable jobs during this age include farming, trading, teaching, and preaching.

Narrator 2: It is a point of pride for successful men to be involved in programs that are meant to benefit the less fortunate.

Narrator 1: Thomas Gallaudet is still a young man without a career, but he has graduated from Yale University and Andover Theological Seminary. He also briefly studied law.

Narrator 2: Looking out the window of his mother's living room, he watches his younger siblings play in the yard.

Narrator 3: One child is not playing with the rest. She glances from time to time at the others but otherwise ignores them. She is gathering flowers and weaving them into a wreath.

Thomas: I wonder why she does not play with the others?

Narrator 1: Thomas opens the window.

Thomas: Teddy!

Teddy: What?

Thomas: Come here for a minute.

Narrator 2: The young boy willingly comes over. With him is Edward, who is curious to see what Thomas wants.

Thomas: Who is that girl?

American History Reader's Theater © 2004 Creative Teaching Press

Teddy: Oh, that's Alice! You know. She is Mr. Cogswell's younger daughter.

Thomas: Why don't you play with her?

Teddy: She's nice actually, but you can't talk to her. Sometimes she plays with us, but after awhile . . . I don't know. I guess she gets tired of not being able to understand.

Thomas: She does not understand you?

Teddy: She can't. She is deaf.

Thomas: She is deaf? I don't remember that.

Teddy: I don't think they knew when she was really little. They just thought she was slow to talk. She is really quite clever.

Thomas: How do you know?

Edward: Well, you can draw a picture in the dirt of something you want her to find and she understands perfectly.

Thomas: Can she read?

Teddy: I don't think so. I don't think she goes to school. The schoolmaster said he did not know how to teach a deaf child.

Thomas: It can't be all that different . . . you would just need a simple way to communicate.

Edward: How?

Thomas: I don't know. Maybe with your pictures. Is she shy? Will she come over to me?

Teddy: She is a little shy, but I think she would meet you. Let me go see.

Narrator 2: Teddy runs over to Alice. He points to his brother and pulls on her elbow in his direction.

Narrator 3: Alice is curious to see Thomas. She knows that the other children are fond of him.

Narrator 1: Thomas leaves the living room window and walks around to the door leading to the porch. He spies his hat sitting on a table by the door and has an idea.

Narrator 2: He puts the hat on his head.

Thomas: How do you do, Alice?

Narrator 3: Alice is silent, but she smiles at him.

American History Reader's Theater © 2004 Creative Teaching Press

THOMAS AND ALICE

Narrator 1:   Thomas sits on the bottom porch step. He picks up a stick and points to his hat.

Thomas: This is how you write "hat."

Narrator 1:   Thomas draws H-A-T in the dirt. Then he points to the hat again.

Thomas: This is a hat.

Narrator 1:   He gives the hat to Alice and rubs out the first word. Then he points to the hat in Alice's hand and writes H-A-T again in the dirt.

Thomas: Hat!

Narrator 1:   He does this again and again.

Narrator 3:   Alice is pleased. She understands. She smiles. The next time Thomas writes H-A-T, she hands the hat to him and points first to the word and then to the hat.

Narrator 2:   Emily notices and comes over to see what is happening.

Narrator 1:   One more time he writes H-A-T. This time he pulls out his handkerchief. He holds up the handkerchief and the hat and raises his eyebrows as if to ask, "Which is it?"

Narrator 3:   Alice points to the hat.

Teddy, Edward, and Emily: Yay! Good work, Alice!

Narrator 3:   Alice cannot hear them, but she can see that the others are pleased with her answer.

Thomas: What a fine game we have going here. Let's see what else you can understand, Alice.

Narrator 3:   Alice taps Thomas on the arm. She stops smiling.

Thomas: What's the matter, Alice?

Narrator 3:   She rubs out the word in the dirt. She points to herself. She lifts her eyebrows. She points to the dirt.

Thomas: Oh, Alice, you are clever, aren't you?

Narrator 1:   Thomas writes in the dirt A-L-I-C-E. Then he writes H-A-T. He points to the long word and to Alice. He points to the short word and the hat.

Narrator 3:   Alice understands. She grins. She takes Thomas' stick and copies the letters of her own name and then points to herself.

American History Reader's Theater © 2004 Creative Teaching Press

THOMAS AND ALICE

Emily: Alice! Alice! You can write your name! Father will be so excited! Mother will not believe it! I wonder what else she can write?

Thomas: I suspect she can write anything if we teach it to her.

Emily: Here, Alice. This is my name!

Narrator 2: The children take turns writing their names in the dirt and pointing to themselves.

Narrator 3: Now there are a lot of new words in the dirt. It is kind of confusing. But Alice knows which word is hers.

Emily: Let's start over!

Narrator 1: Emily erases all the words. Just then, an older man enters the yard.

Emily: Father! Come here! See what Thomas has done with Alice!

Mr. Cogswell: Good to have you back, Thomas. What game has Alice taught you?

Thomas: We have come up with something together, sir. Watch this.

Narrator 1: He hands the hat and stick to Alice.

Narrator 3: Alice writes in the earth H-A-T.

Mr. Cogswell: Oh, my!

Narrator 1: The older man bends down to hug his daughter . . .

Narrator 3: . . . but she wriggles out of his grasp. She holds up the stick proudly and points to herself.

Mr. Cogswell: You?

Narrator 3: Alice slowly and carefully spells out her own name in the dirt. She pauses halfway through.

Narrator 2: Thomas writes the letter in the dirt.

Narrator 3: Alice nods and copies the letter into her own name, then finishes her name.

Narrator 1: The children applaud for her again.

Narrator 3: Alice opens her arms for her father. She is ready for that hug now.

Narrator 2: But Mr. Cogswell cannot move. He is overcome with emotion. Tears run down his face.

American History Reader's Theater © 2004 Creative Teaching Press

THOMAS AND ALICE

Thomas: I firmly believe your daughter can be educated, Mr. Cogswell.

Mr. Cogswell: Do you have the time to do it?

Thomas: I would be honored!

Mr. Cogswell: There are many others like her, you know.

Thomas: Then we must find the best way to teach her and open a school for them all.

Mr. Cogswell: If you would direct it, I would gladly fund it. There are two other families with deaf children here but no schools for the deaf anywhere in America.

Thomas: We could start as I have with Alice, but there must be a better way.

Mr. Cogswell: Would you be willing to travel? I have heard there are very successful schools in England and France. If I sent you there for a few months, you could gain some training . . .

Thomas: . . . and return to start the new school by this time next year!

Emily: And Alice could learn to read and write!

Mr. Cogswell: Thomas, will you do it?

Thomas: Yes. Alice is quite clever and really wants to learn. I think we owe her the education she wants. If there are others like her, we cannot deny them the opportunity.

Mr. Cogswell: Let's go make plans then.

Emily: Come, let's finish our game.

Narrator 3: Alice runs off with the others to play.

American History Reader's Theater © 2004 Creative Teaching Press

RELATED LESSON

My Name Is...

OBJECTIVE

Learn to sign a sentence in American Sign Language.

ACTIVITY

Create a center with an **online American Sign Language dictionary** bookmarked for students (see below for some resources), copies of the **Finger Spelling Alphabet reproducible (page 41),** and a few **print resources** if they are available. (Paperback ASL dictionaries are inexpensive and available at most bookstores.) Challenge students to research the signs to communicate MY NAME IS and then learn the finger spelling of their own first and last name. Have students record their information on an **ASL Worksheet (page 42).** Give students time to practice introducing themselves to a partner. Then, invite them to introduce themselves in sign to the class.

You might find the following Web sites helpful:
Finger spelling dictionary: where.com/scott.net/asl/abc.html
Animated dictionary: commtechlab.msu.edu/sites/aslweb/browser.htm*

Alternatively, you can provide students with the *American Sign Language Dictionary* by Martin L.A. Sternberg, Ed.D. (Multimedia 2000, Inc.) on CD-Rom.

*This site requires Quicktime4.

Finger Spelling Alphabet

Directions: Use the following signs to spell out names of people and places.

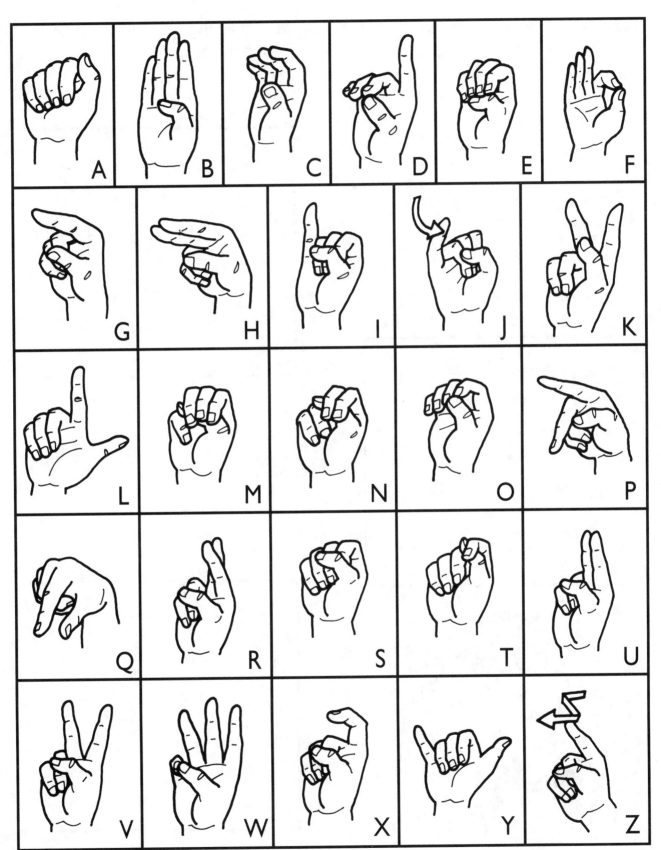

Name_____   Date _____

ASL Worksheet

Directions: Draw a picture for each word to help you remember the sign for the word. On the back, draw a sketch of your fingers for each letter of your first name.

MY

NAME

IS

Hi!

42   The First School for the Deaf in America

American History Reader's Theater © 2004 Creative Teaching Press

SITTING BULL

AMERICAN HISTORY

VOCABULARY

Discuss each of the following words with students. Then, have students choose one of the words to research in a print or online encyclopedia or dictionary. Have students create a chart that teaches the class more about that word.

count coup: to tag the enemy in a battle, alive or dead

cradleboard: a wooden cradle that a baby could be bundled in and hung from a tree or worn on the mother's back to keep the baby safe and secure

impatient: unwilling to wait a reasonable length of time

winter count: an oral retelling of important stories that occurred in the winter; it was often accompanied by a large buffalo skin on which were painted illustrations that depicted the stories

BACKGROUND

Sitting Bull spends an afternoon with his family as a child. Factual elements of this story include his childhood name and that of his father. The other names are in alignment with Sioux naming traditions of the time (including giving young children names they would want to grow out of, such as Hiccups and Slow). Sitting Bull was good with animals, brave in battle, and an excellent hunter. He was considered generous, friendly, and possessed a good sense of humor.

Narrator

Slow: 9-year-old Sioux boy who
will one day be Sitting Bull

Laughs Loudly: Slow's mother

Returns Again: Slow's father

Dances: 12-year-old sister

Hiccups: 8-year-old sister

FLUENCY INSTRUCTION

Have students discuss the ages of the characters to help them reflect the maturity level in their reading. When you read aloud the script for students, have them listen for the following:

- The pace of the reading speeds up when children are excited. Have students name at least three places where the reading pace will pick up in this script.

- The pace slows down when someone is being earnest. Have students notice how carefully you enunciate and pace your words when you speak Slow's lines addressed to his father.

- Your pitch is ever so slightly lower for the older daughter Dances than for Hiccups. Point out that Hiccups is younger than Dances and the actors with those roles will need to find a way to show that with their voices.

COMPREHENSION

After you read aloud the script, ask students these questions:

1. What item does Slow decide he needs to make at the end of the scene?

2. How did Slow earn his name as a baby?

3. Name one example of a time when Slow's patience paid off.

4. Does Slow's name still fit him now? Explain your answer.

5. In what ways does Slow hope to make his father and family proud?

SLOW AND STEADY

PARTS

Narrator
Slow: 9-year-old Sioux boy who
    will one day be Sitting Bull
Laughs Loudly: Slow's mother
Returns Again: Slow's father
Dances: 12-year-old sister
Hiccups: 8-year-old sister

Narrator: It is mid-July on the plains of America in an area that would one day be Minnesota. A large extended family of Lakota Sioux are camped near their hunting grounds.

Returns Again: What are you doing, Son?

Slow: I am painting a story on my little sister's cradleboard.

Returns Again: Is that an opossum?

Slow: No, Father, it is a mountain lion to show her bravery!

Returns Again: Keep working on it, Son. Your mountain lion looks an awful lot like an opossum.

Narrator: The Lakota hunted buffalo and moved often. An entire village could be ready to go in fifteen minutes. The people admired two traits above all others: generosity and bravery.

Returns Again: Now it looks like a . . . I don't know. I have never seen anything that looks like that.

Slow: I am not done, Father. Be patient.

Returns Again: Maybe your sister's cradleboard does not need a new painting.

Slow: I want to paint the stories for the winter count, Father. I have to practice. Now look at it. Does it look like a mountain lion?

Returns Again: Oh! Look at that! It kind of does look like a mountain lion! Good job.

Laughs Loudly: Here come the girls. I can start dinner now.

Slow: What are we having for dinner?

Narrator: Slow's sisters show him the food they gathered.

Slow: That will go well with the rabbit I caught!

Returns Again: It won't be long before you are catching bigger animals than that for the family.

Slow: I want to hunt buffalo, Father.

American History Reader's Theater © 2004 Creative Teaching Press

SLOW AND STEADY

Returns Again: You are getting bigger. Last week you helped the bigger boys bring down a few calves.

Slow: But I want to get us a grown buffalo. I want to bring honor to the family.

Hiccups: Bring me a buffalo, Brother. I will make you new moccasins.

Slow: With quills and beads on them?

Hiccups: Maybe, if it is a really large buffalo!

Laughs Loudly: She will only paint it if it is a small buffalo.

Returns Again: Maybe, if you are lucky, she will put your opossum on it.

Slow: It is not an opossum! Look, Hiccups, what is this animal?

Hiccups: On the cradleboard? It is, uh, I am not sure, but it looks a little like a mountain lion.

Returns Again: Oh, Hiccups, you got it right. Now Slow will be Slow with a Big Head.

Dances: What do you expect when he is the only boy? He is spoiled.

Laughs Loudly: What? Slow brought you three rabbits for your supper, Dances.

Dances: I am only teasing, Mother. Everyone knows Slow makes us proud.

Slow: I am tired of my name! I want to make you so proud that I earn a name for a man.

Laughs Loudly: That will come in time, Slow.

Hiccups: Tell me again how Slow got his name.

Returns Again: "Come along, Baby!" we would say.

Laughs Loudly: But he would not answer. He would stand and smile as if to say, "Come get me! I don't want to walk."

Returns Again: "Hurry and eat, Little One!" we would say.

Laughs Loudly: He would slowly pop the fruit in his mouth berry by berry.

Returns Again: "Run and catch the ball, Baby!" we would call.

Laughs Loudly: He would laugh and sit down in the grass and wait for us to bring it to him.

Returns Again: So we called him Slow.

Slow: But now I am older. I am not always last.

American History Reader's Theater © 2004 Creative Teaching Press

Slow and Steady

Laughs Loudly: No, you are no longer my Slow Turtle. Now you are slow to get angry, slow to give up, and slow to grow impatient.

Dances: You did a great job with your horse, Slow. I was impressed.

Slow: He is a good pony. He is very strong.

Hiccups: I did not think he could be tamed, but you did not give up on him.

Returns Again: It turns out that slow is a very good speed for some things.

Slow: Like getting to know your pony!

Narrator: Slow holds up the cradleboard.

Slow: It is all done!

Laughs Loudly: Very nice, Son. I like the designs you painted next to your mountain lion.

Slow: I made her a doll, too. It will give her something to do so she does not wander into the fire.

Returns Again: As soon as she can hold it well, I am sure she will like her brother's gift.

Slow: Father, what if I am always Slow?

Returns Again: You aren't always slow. You are really quite swift on that grey pony.

Slow: No, I mean, what if I never earn any honors and I am always *called* Slow?

Returns Again: Then we will cope with that when it happens. But it will not happen. You are my only son and although there are others who move more quickly, there are few who move more thoughtfully.

Laughs Loudly: When you do decide to move quickly, you are very fast and very brave.

Slow: I want a name like Father's: Returns Again to Strike the Enemy!

Dances: Then you will have to join the war party when they go out!

Laughs Loudly: But not yet. You need to grow a few more inches.

Hiccups: You need to weigh a little more. I do not think it counts to count coup on the enemy if they cannot see you coming.

Slow: I am not that small!

Hiccups: I am just kidding!

American History Reader's Theater © 2004 Creative Teaching Press

SLOW AND STEADY

Laughs Loudly: Do not tease your brother, dear.

Dances: Maybe you will be called Many Horns for all the buffalo you will catch us!

Hiccups: Oh! I would like that. I could be Many Shoes for all the moccasins I could make us then.

Dances: Then we would need to find you a husband named Many Horses so he can carry them all for you!

Laughs Loudly: That would be a good name, too! Many Horses would be a name won when you stole them out from under the noses of the Crow!

Slow: Maybe I will be First to the Enemy!

Dances: Then you had better be a swift rider!

Hiccups: Or you will become Knocked Off Pony.

Laughs Loudly: Hiccups!

Hiccups: What?!? Hey, where are you going, Slow? Come back, I was just kidding!

Slow: I know you were kidding, Hiccups. But I am off to work on my new name! And for that, I will need new arrows.

Returns Again: I will check your work when you are done, Slow.

Slow: Thank you, Father!

Narrator: The family settled into preparations for the evening meal as Slow worked on a new set of arrows. They did not know he would one day be Sitting Bull, but they did know he would one day make them proud.

American History Reader's Theater © 2004 Creative Teaching Press

RELATED LESSON

The Sioux

OBJECTIVE
Gather information about the Sioux.

ACTIVITY

Give each student a copy of the **Sioux** and **What Did You Learn?** reproducibles (pages **50–51**). Review the questions on the What Did You Learn? reproducible so students can set a purpose for reading. Have students read along as you read aloud the Sioux reproducible. Then, divide the class into pairs, and have each pair answer the questions. Discuss the answers as a class.

ANSWERS

1. The Europeans introduced the horse to the Sioux.
2. The Sioux depended on the buffalo for food and materials.
3. Women cooked, cared for the children, and were in charge of putting up and taking down the tipis.
4. Sioux warfare was used to defend the land and get horses. Men would count coup by touching the enemy.
5. The goal of Sioux warfare was to get horses and defend the land.
6. The home of the Sioux tribe today is in South Dakota.

Sioux

Directions: Read the passage and then answer the questions on the What Did You Learn? page.

The Sioux Nation moved from the Southeast to the Plains in the 1500s. When Europeans brought the horse to America, the Sioux quickly adapted the animal to their lifestyle. They became even more mobile and adept at hunting buffalo. The Sioux of early America were proud warriors and excellent hunters. They valued generosity, wisdom, and bravery. Today, members of the Sioux tribe live throughout the United States.

Life for the Sioux in the 1800s revolved around the buffalo. Buffalos gave them meat to eat. Buffalo skins were used to make tipis and warm, strong clothing. Women cooked, cared for the children, and were in charge of setting up and taking down the tipis. Women worked together. An entire family group could be ready to move to a new location in 15 minutes. Men hunted and participated in warfare.

Sioux warfare was not like modern warfare. The Sioux wanted to get horses and keep the land around the buffalo. It was brave to risk death. The men and boys would "count coup" by being the first to touch an enemy—alive or dead. It was like a grown-up game of tag where the warrior wanted to steal the other team's horses and frighten the other team so they ran away. People did die sometimes, but a good battle ended with the Sioux capturing all the horses, the other tribe running away, and no one killed.

For a long time after the settlers arrived, the Sioux were not treated well. They were moved to new land where nothing would grow well. The Sioux were forced into poverty. Important customs and language were lost. It was very

difficult to be a Sioux in America. Today, the home of the Sioux tribe is in South Dakota, but the Siouan people live everywhere in America.

American History Reader's Theater © 2004 Creative Teaching Press

What Did You Learn?

Directions: Read the questions. Use the information on the Sioux page to answer each question in a complete sentence.

1. What animal did the Europeans introduce to the Sioux?

2. What animal did the Sioux depend on for food and materials?

3. Name two things that Sioux women did.

4. Describe Sioux warfare.

5. What was the goal of going to war?

6. Where is the home of the Sioux today?

THE
PONY
EXPRESS

AMERICAN
HISTORY

Vocabulary

Discuss each of the following words with students. Then, have students discuss how they could find more information about the meaning of each word.

breeches: pants

covering for us: preventing misbehavior from being discovered

ground: to punish by keeping home

hedges: large bushes often used to border a yard or create a sense of privacy

mending: sewing

opportunity: chance

orphan: a child without a living parent

Background

Mrs. Hudson's two oldest children are both eager to join the newly organized Pony Express. A heated discussion between the siblings results in a race to see which is the better rider. The local manager of the Pony Express witnesses the race and rewards the winner with a job offer. The text from the ad accurately reflects the actual ads run for the Pony Express, which ran for about 18 months before the opening of the transcontinental railroad. The ad does not reflect the actual riders hired though. (Maybe the ad writers overestimated the availability of orphans with strong riding skills?) Most riders were around 20 years old, but the youngest was 11. Most were not orphans. They earned $100 a month and rode for about 75 miles (121 km), changing horses every 10 to 15 miles (17 to 24 km). The route was from St. Joseph, Missouri, to Sacramento, California.

PARTS

- Narrator 1
- Narrator 2
- Narrator 3
- Mr. Galloway: Director of the Pony Express
- ★ Mrs. Hudson: mother of seven boys and one girl
- Milo: 16-year-old boy
- Ruth: 15-year-old girl
- Ben: 13-year-old boy
- Andrew: 12-year-old boy
- Chester: 10-year-old boy
- Billy: 8-year-old boy
- ⚜ Joe: 6-year-old boy
- ⚜ Mark: 5-year-old boy

FLUENCY INSTRUCTION

Have students discuss the ages of the characters to help them reflect the maturity level in their reading. When you read aloud the script for students, have them listen for the following:

- The overall pace of the reading is fast. These are mostly children, they are from a tight-knit family that knows each other well, and they are comfortable teasing and talking to each other.
- The pitch lowers when the children talk to their mother. They respect her. There is no teasing in their voices when they speak to her.
- Your pitch is ever so slightly lower when you deliver the lines from mother to daughter in which she offers some sympathy for her daughter's desire to ride and travel.
- Your voice rises when it expresses anger.

COMPREHENSION

After you read aloud the script, ask students these questions:

1. In what state does the story takes place?

2. Summarize what happens in the story.

3. How can you show that the word *orphans* in Billy's line on the first page of your script is a question? What do you think an orphan is?

4. Why do you think the owners of the Pony Express were particularly interested in orphans?

5. Would you have been interested in a Pony Express job? Explain why or why not.

PONY EXPRESS

PARTS

Narrator 1
Narrator 2
Narrator 3
Mr. Galloway: Director of the
    Pony Express
Mrs. Hudson: mother of seven
    boys and one girl
Milo: 16-year-old boy
Ruth: 15-year-old girl
Ben: 13-year-old boy
Andrew: 12-year-old boy
Chester: 10-year-old boy
Billy: 8-year-old boy
Joe: 6-year-old boy
Mark: 5-year-old boy

Narrator 1: It is mid-May and the children from a Missouri family are gathered around a flyer posted in the general store window.

Ruth: Move over! You are on my foot!

Billy: Ow! That is your elbow in my ribs!

Narrator 2: The town is small. The main street is two blocks long and consists of a general store, a tavern, a town hall that doubles as a jail when the need arises, and a small school building.

Mark: What's it say? What's it say?

Joe: Something about the Pony Express!

Chester: It says that they need riders!

Andrew: It says they want orphans.

Billy: Orphans? That leaves us out.

Milo: Oh, they don't mean it.

Mark: Read me the whole thing, Ruth.

Narrator 3: Ruth reads the flyer to the others.

Ruth: "Wanted. Young, skinny, wiry fellows. Not over 18. Must be expert riders. Willing to risk death daily. Orphans preferred."

Billy: That leaves you out, Ruth! Ow! Why'd you hit me?

Milo: I am going to apply. I am a "fellow."

Ben: You are? Well, then I am, too!

American History Reader's Theater © 2004 Creative Teaching Press

PONY EXPRESS

Ruth, Andrew, Chester, Billy, Joe, Mark: Me, too!!

Mark: You can't Ruth! You're a girl!

Ruth: You're five, Mark. If you can ride to California, then I should be able to make it to Mexico!

Chester: Do you think the Pony Express goes that far?

Andrew: No, Chester, and from here, you don't even go to California.

Joe: Everyone knows the Pony Express goes to California!

Andrew: But it isn't the same rider the whole way.

Joe: Is it the same horse?

Ruth: No, Joe. You can't ride a horse that fast for more than about ten miles.

Milo: Maybe fifteen if the land is flat and the weather is nice.

Ruth: You really could go, Milo.

Milo: Sorry you can't, Ruth.

Ruth: Maybe if I cut my hair and borrowed your smallest trousers!

Milo: Mama needs your help with the boys, even if you could pull it off.

Ben: Mr. Galloway would recognize you, Ruth.

Ruth: I can ride better than all of you.

Milo: What?!?

Ruth: I can. I'm faster and I stay on better over jumps.

Milo: I think that sounds like a challenge boys!

Mark: Mama's not gonna like this.

Billy: OK, to make it fair, I'll pick the horses!

Ruth: No, I'm riding Sheba.

Billy: I was going to pick her for you anyway. Milo, you can ride Hunter.

Milo: Since we are going for speed and jumps, I say we start in front of the schoolhouse.

Ruth: Right, we go as far as the town limits.

American History Reader's Theater © 2004 Creative Teaching Press

PONY EXPRESS

Chester: I'm going to watch for Mother. If I see her, I'll give the signal.

Ruth: Thanks for covering for us, Chester.

Chester: I am not covering for you. I am just giving the signal. I do not need a whipping if Ruth tears her dress and Milo makes our strongest horse lame.

Ruth: He won't hurt the horse. He might lose the race, but he wouldn't hurt that horse.

Narrator 1: Ruth and Milo get on their horses and steer the animals towards the other end of the street.

Narrator 2: As they do, a man comes around from the back of the store.

Mr. Galloway: A race?

Mark: Ruth says she's a better rider than Milo.

Joe: Milo wants to ride for the Pony Express!

Billy: So does Ruth, but they'll never let her because she isn't an orphan.

Andrew: Mark, do you know what an orphan is?

Mark: No.

Andrew: Just forget the orphan thing. I don't think it really matters if you can ride.

Mr. Galloway: I do not think your mother would let the Pony Express hire her daughter to ride 75 miles a few times a week.

Andrew: Don't tell that to Ruth!

Mark: But Mama might let Milo go if the rest of us agreed to do his chores.

Mr. Galloway: Do you think you could do his chores?

Mark: Well, I could milk his cows.

Ben: Sure, we could all help. He would be home some days anyway.

Mr. Galloway: Maybe I had better stay to watch the race. Mark, once the kids have started, you should probably go get your mother.

Andrew: I think Milo will win. He really is the faster rider.

Ben: That depends, Andrew. Ruth can get Sheba to jump anything, and sometimes Hunter balks.

American History Reader's Theater © 2004 Creative Teaching Press

PONY EXPRESS

Chester: They're going to go over the schoolhouse hedges.

Mr. Galloway: Oooh, the schoolmaster will not like that.

Narrator 3: The door to the store opens.

Mrs. Hudson: Where are Milo and Ruth? I asked you all to stay put.

Narrators 1, 2, and 3: Chester whistles loudly. Ruth and Milo urge their horses into a run.

Narrator 1: Milo takes a slight lead, but as both horses jump the schoolhouse hedges, Sheba lands ahead.

Mrs. Hudson: Are those MY children? What on earth is going on here?

Mr. Galloway: I do believe, Mrs. Hudson, that your children are trying out for the Pony Express.

Narrator 2: The horses reach the other end of the school yard and jump the hedges on that side. They turn down the street that passes behind the general store, riding faster and faster.

Narrator 3: They are neck and neck as they ride down four blocks and turn north back to Main Street.

Mrs. Hudson: Please hire my daughter, Mr. Galloway. Otherwise I may have to ground her until her wedding day for this.

Mr. Galloway: [laughing] I can't do that, Mrs. Hudson, but I do see that she rides well!

Narrator 1: In the final stretch, Milo's horse has the advantage of speed and the two horses pass the general store with his horse just ahead.

Mr. Galloway: Would you give your permission for your son to go?

Mrs. Hudson: Only if you promise to take the rest as they grow older.

Mr. Galloway: I will take that as a yes. Let me go talk to your son. Good luck with your daughter!

Narrator 2: The two children, out of breath, run up to the porch of the general store.

Ruth: That was close! We should go again! I know I could beat you on a second round!

Mrs. Hudson: Ruth Ann Hudson, you are not going anywhere!

Ruth: Oh! Mama! How long have you been there?

Mrs. Hudson: Long enough to see the whole thing.

Ruth: I'm sorry, Mama. I am. I just . . .

PONY EXPRESS

Mrs. Hudson: I know, Ruth. I do. I remember what it feels like to ride like that, too.

Ruth: Mr. Galloway is talking to Milo. I guess he is going to be a Pony Express rider then.

Mrs. Hudson: Ruth, you will find your own way to California, if that is what you want. Just wait your turn and the opportunity will present itself in a way that is right for you.

Ruth: Do you really think so?

Mrs. Hudson: Yes, I do. And it will not be by jumping horses over the schoolhouse hedges, so do not let me see you practicing that skill again.

Ruth: What skills do you think I will need?

Mrs. Hudson: None that you do not already have. But I think I am going to have you practice your mending skills.

Ruth: Mama!

Mrs. Hudson: No arguing. You tore your best skirt. You can fix that one and then make each of your younger brothers new breeches.

Ruth: That will take forever!

Mrs. Hudson: Since you will not be allowed to leave my sight for the next month, you will have plenty of time.

Chester: [singsong] Ruth is in trouble.

Mrs. Hudson: Yes, she is, and so are you. Honestly. Why didn't one of you come to get me? Someone could have been hurt!

Narrator 3: Milo runs up to the general store porch.

Milo: Mom! Mr. Galloway offered me a job! It's $100 a month! I'm to ride on the days that Johnny Fry is away. Mama, can I take the job?

Mrs. Hudson: Yes. You be careful, Milo. We still need you at home when you can be there. I'm proud of you, but use good sense.

Mark: You will have to tell us all about your rides when you are home!

Milo: I will! Maybe Ruth will even help me write it down?

Ruth: Of course I will. I can do that to help.

Mrs. Hudson: We had better go home to tell Father about today's events!

American History Reader's Theater © 2004 Creative Teaching Press

RELATED LESSONS

Transcontinental Communication

OBJECTIVE
Investigate the Pony Express and the transcontinental railroad.

ACTIVITY

Provide students with **online and print resources related to the Pony Express and the transcontinental railroad.** Give each student an **East to West reproducible (page 60).** Have students choose a topic (either the Pony Express or the transcontinental railroad) and answer the questions on the reproducible. Then, have them use the information they gathered to create an educational poster for the class.

Character Building

OBJECTIVE
Research and develop a character who rode for the Pony Express or worked for the transcontinental railroad.

ACTIVITY

Have students use **the information they gathered from the Transcontinental Communication activity** to help them develop an imaginary character who rode for the Pony Express or transcontinental railroad. Have them include

- a character name typical of the era
- what town he or she was from
- what portion of the route their character worked
- what his or her job responsibilities included
- the character's age
- how he or she decided to take the job
- any other information that helps make their character seem real

Have students write up a description of the character they developed. Then, give students **drawing paper,** and have them create a portrait of their character in work clothes. Display the finished pieces in a bulletin board display titled *We Are On the Move!*

Name_____   Date _____

East to West

Directions: Use books or online Web sites to answer the following questions for your topic.

Topic: (circle one)   **Pony Express**   **Transcontinental Railroad**

Question	Answer
Describe this method of getting from the East to the West.	
What kinds of materials did it carry? For example, could a family travel to the West Coast using this method of transportation? Could mail? Explain.	
How long did it take to get from the East to the West by this method of transportation?	
What was the earliest date you could use this method of transportation to get a letter or package from the East to the West?	

American History Reader's Theater © 2004 Creative Teaching Press

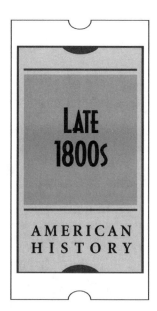

LATE
1800s

AMERICAN
HISTORY

VOCABULARY

Discuss each of the following words with students. Then, have students sort the words by parts of speech.

dense: thick or heavy (adjective)

hinges: two interlocking pieces of metal that connect with a pin to hold a door to its frame (noun)

locksmith: a person who makes and repairs locks and keys (noun)

padlock: a detachable lock with a movable semicircular bar at the top, the free end of which is usually passed through a hasp and then locked shut (noun)

sliver: a thin, strip of wood or metal (noun)

wispy: lightweight and slightly see-through (adjective)

BACKGROUND

Harry Houdini, a traveling magician, has made his reputation on amazing escape tricks from locks. Today, he gets stuck in his bedroom at the boardinghouse where he and his wife are staying. Local children come to his rescue. At this time in history, the toilet had been invented, but it was still very uncommon. A boardinghouse like this might have had a room for a bathtub, but it might also have had a small washtub that was in the person's room. Children played baseball, but probably a girl Barb's age would have been helping her mother and not playing the game. Houdini did travel with his wife and she was part of the show.

★ Narrator 1
Narrator 2
Narrator 3
Houdini: 30-year-old magician
Bess: Houdini's wife
Mrs. Stengl: hotel owner
Henry: 10-year-old son of the
    hotel owner
Rich: 9-year-old son of the
    hotel owner
James: 9-year-old friend
Leo: 9-year-old friend
Barb: 8-year-old daughter of the
    hotel owner
❀ Nancy: 8-year-old friend

FLUENCY INSTRUCTION

Have students discuss the ages of the characters to help them reflect the maturity level in their reading. When you read aloud the script for students, have them listen for the following:

• The pace of the reading speeds up when children are excited. Have students name at least two places where the reading pace will pick up in this script.

• The pace slows down when someone is trying to explain something important to someone else. Have students find one place in the script where this happens.

• Your pace and pitch are fairly steady for any of the narrator lines. These lines usually describe activity, and while you avoid monotone, which would be boring, you also avoid conveying too much emotion since the narrator is not part of the scene.

• Your voice falls at the end of a line that contains an ellipsis such as on the line *Houdini: Oh, no . . . .*

COMPREHENSION

After you read aloud the script, ask students these questions:

1. How did Harry Houdini get stuck in his room?

2. Describe the house in which Houdini is staying.

3. How do they eventually solve the problem of the broken lock?

4. Why does Barb whisper to the others *I got it!* and then yell to her mother *Hey, Mom, should we check on the soap?*

5. Do you think this scene could really have happened? Why or why not?

HOUDINI IS STUCK!

American History Reader's Theater © 2004 Creative Teaching Press

PARTS

Narrator 1
Narrator 2
Narrator 3
Houdini: 30-year-old magician
Bess: Houdini's wife
Mrs. Stengl: hotel owner
Henry: 10-year-old son of the
    hotel owner
Rich: 9-year-old son of the
    hotel owner
James: 9-year-old friend
Leo: 9-year-old friend
Barb: 8-year-old daughter of the
    hotel owner
Nancy: 8-year-old friend

Narrator 1: It is late morning and the small country hotel is quiet. Sunlight streams in through a small window at the end of the hall. Wispy curtains flutter in the spring breeze.

Narrator 2: It is 1902 and most of the rooms in this large house are rented to members of a traveling act. A small man with dark, wavy hair heads down the hall to his room to shave and prepare for the day.

Narrator 3: He carries in his hands a bowl of steaming water. The old house has no bathroom, as we know it today.

Narrator 1: He shuts the door behind him and turns the lock for privacy. As he does so, the lock sticks. He jiggles it impatiently. With a loud snapping noise, the lock suddenly clicks into place.

Houdini: Oh, no . . .

Narrator 2: The man tries to turn the lock back to open. The lock's knob will not turn. It is jammed.

Narrator 3: As he tries to think what to do, we hear the sound of pounding feet.

Mrs. Stengl: Richard John Stengl, how many times have I told you no running in the house?

Rich: Sorry!

James: All the doors are closed! Are you full today?

Rich: Yes. Shhh. We should probably try to be quiet.

Narrator 2: A door down the hall opens.

Henry: Have you seen my glove? I can't find it anywhere.

HOUDINI IS STUCK!

Rich: I think Barb is using it. She's catcher today.

Henry: I thought she was helping Mom make soap?

Rich: She says she's done already.

Houdini: [coughs] Gentlemen?

James: [whispering] Who was that?

Leo: I think it came from that room!

Rich: Oh! He must want his towels. Sorry, Mr. Houdini! My mom sent me up—uh, can you unlock your door?

Houdini: I do not seem to be able to.

Narrator 1: There are more footsteps on the stairs.

Barb: What is taking you all so long? Everyone is ready to start the game!

Rich: I need to give the magician his towels, but he says he can't open the door.

Nancy: Magician? Why doesn't he just say "Abracadabra!" and get himself out?

Bess: [laughing, behind the door] I do not think magic would work on this ordinary door lock.

Barb: How many people are in there?!?

Houdini: Just my wife and I. But we have a show in an hour!

Henry: What kind of show?

Bess: We stand outside the main tent and perform magic tricks. If you can get us out, we will give you each a free ticket to the show.

All Kids: Great!

Leo: I will go get your mom!

Houdini: Wait!

Leo: You want me to wait?

Houdini: It's just … my act …

American History Reader's Theater © 2004 Creative Teaching Press

HOUDINI IS STUCK!

Bess:	My husband is trying to say that it would be best if few people knew that the great Harry Houdini was stuck in a locked bedroom.
Houdini:	In my act, I escape from all manner of locks!
James:	If people found out you cannot escape from a simple bedroom lock, it could ruin your career.
Houdini:	[wailing] It is not the same!
Bess:	This is a broken lock. Harry works with regular padlocks and handcuffs. None of them are broken. We show the crowd how well they work before each show.
Henry:	[peering through the keyhole] Yes . . . I think I see the problem. There is a piece of metal that is broken off . . .
Mrs. Stengl:	[calling up the stairs] Kids, are you bothering our guests?
All Kids:	No, ma'am! [to each other] Shhhhhh!
Leo:	How can we get him out? Maybe get a locksmith?
Houdini and Bess:	No!
Bess:	I am sure there is another way.
Barb:	What about those screws?
Houdini:	Yes! That is the way to think! The screws that hold the lock plate on the door!
Nancy:	They are a funny shape.
James:	Nancy is right. You are going to have a hard time getting those out.
Bess:	A funny shape?
Rich:	Yes, I think they are kind of old.

[The group falls silent for a moment.]

Nancy:	But there are other screws!
Rich:	Good eye, Nancy!
Henry:	What screws?
Rich:	She means the pins in the hinges!

Houdini: Good girl! So clever!

Mrs. Stengl: What are you kids up to? [muttering] I am coming up to check on you. It is too quiet.

Barb: [whispering] I got it! [loudly] Hey, Mom, should we check on the soap?

Mrs. Stengl: Soap? The soap is fine. But come down here and set the table for dinner.

Barb: [groaning, quietly] I'll go. You guys hurry up and get them out! It will only be about five minutes before Mom will want us all down to eat!

James: We need something sharp.

Nancy: Like a needle?

Leo: No, it needs to be bigger, flatter, something we can use to pry the pin up.

Henry: Or . . . we could knock it out by pushing it up from the bottom!

Houdini: A heavy book?

Nancy: A baseball?

Rich: Hey! Let me see that.

Narrator 2: Rich takes the dense leather ball and swings it up hard against the bottom of the door hinge. With a pop, the thin metal pin shoots halfway out of the hinge.

Narrator 3: Henry grabs the top of the pin and wiggles it side to side until it slides the rest of the way out of the hinge.

Bess: What is happening?

Nancy: They are getting it! The first pin is out! Only one more to go!

Houdini: Hurry! Hurry!

Mrs. Stengl: Wash up, boys!

James: Let me do the next one!

Narrator 1: James swings the leather ball against the bottom of the remaining door hinge. As before, the pin pops up halfway out of the hinge.

Narrator 2: Again, Henry pulls the pin the rest of the way from the hinge.

Houdini Is Stuck!

Henry: OK, Mr. Houdini. Be very, very quiet! Push against the other side of the door!

Houdini: Stand back just in case!

Narrator 3: Harry Houdini, the greatest escape artist of all time, knocks gently against the door, shaking it carefully loose of the door frame. He is free!

Bess: Put the door back quickly, Harry!

Narrator 1: Now that the door is free, Houdini shakes it carefully and the troublesome sliver of metal shakes loose. He quickly pushes the latch back into the lock.

Houdini: Maybe later today one of you should suggest that your mother look at the lock before someone else gets stuck.

Henry: I will be sure to, Mr. Houdini.

Rich: Here are your towels!

Houdini: Just in time to wash up! Thanks, kids. My wife and I owe you one! Meet us at the tent after dinner for your tickets.

All Kids: Thanks!

American History Reader's Theater © 2004 Creative Teaching Press

RELATED LESSON

Entertainment

OBJECTIVE
Research how children in the early 1900s entertained themselves and give an oral presentation of learned materials.

ACTIVITY

Give each student a **Let Me Entertain You reproducible (page 69)** and access to a variety of **online and print research materials**. Have students use the texts and pictures they find to answer the questions. Then, have students use their answers to write a few paragraphs about how children entertained themselves in the early 20th century. Finally, have students present their report to the class.

LITERATURE LINKS

The following books are not written for children; however, students can learn quite a bit by looking through the pictures to note the toys the children are playing with. Use sticky notes to flag pages you want students to look at.

- *Marbles: A Player's Guide* by Shar Levine and Vicki Scudamore (Sterling)
- *Toys with Nine Lives: A Social History of American Toys* by Andrew McClary (Shoe String Press)
- *Toys (Picture the Past)* by Jane Shuter (Heinnemann)
- *Turn-Of-The-Century Dolls, Toys and Games* by Carl P. Stirn (Dover)

HELPFUL LINKS

Look through the following sites and bookmark those that you think your students may find helpful for their report.

History Channel: www.historychannel.com/exhibits/toys/
turn of the century games and toys: www.emporia.edu/cgps/tales/m95tales.htm
tiddlywinks: www.tiddlywinks.org/collector/agca_grn_article_oct_1996.html
jigsaw puzzles: www.mgcpuzzles.com/mgcpuzzles/puzzle_history/index.htm
wooden toy exhibit: www.pd.astro.it/hosted/bambini/mostra/mostra_i.html
the stage: memory.loc.gov/ammem/vshtml/vshome.html
early animated films: memory.loc.gov/ammem/oahtml/oahome.html

Name_____   Date _____

Let Me Entertain You

Directions: Look through your research materials to answer the following questions about entertainment at the turn of the century. Use the clue words to help you find information.

Clue Words			
baseball	tiddlywinks	models	jigsaw puzzles
dice	vaudeville	slingshots	motion pictures
entertainment	cards	tops	teddy bears
jump rope	dolls	checkers/chess	toy soldiers
Ping-Pong™	jacks	dollhouses	

Questions	Answers
Name toys a boy would play with in the early 1900s.	
Name toys a girl would play with in the early 1900s.	
What kinds of movies might a boy or girl see at this time?	
How were movies in the early 1900s different from today's movies?	
Which toy do you think you would have most enjoyed back then?	

NEW
ORLEANS

AMERICAN
HISTORY

Vocabulary

Discuss each of the following words with students. Then, have students discuss why these words might be important to understanding the script.

humid: damp, with a relatively high amount of moisture in the air

pupil: a student

recruit: a person newly enlisted

satchel: a bag with a large opening for carrying bigger items

tambourine: a small rhythm instrument with one surface like a drum and tiny metal discs that jingle along the edge

tempo: the beat of the music

vibrate: to move back and forth rapidly

Background

Louis Armstrong is a young boy in New Orleans. He will one day become known as one of the greatest jazz musicians in history. Although normally not a troublemaker, some bad decisions on New Year's Eve led to a brief period at a reform school. Here, he is permitted to play with the school band. Armstrong spent most of his childhood supporting his mother and sister in an impoverished section of New Orleans. His introduction to playing music was at the school, but he had listened to music his whole life.

PARTS

Narrator 1
Narrator 2
Narrator 3
Louis Armstrong: 12-year-old boy
Mr. Davis: school band director
Mrs. Johnson: school cook
Willie: 14-year-old boy
Stella: 12-year-old daughter of
    Mr. Davis

FLUENCY INSTRUCTION

Have students discuss the ages of the characters to help them reflect the maturity level in their reading. When you read aloud the script for students, have them listen for the following:

• Stella is younger than everyone else but Louis. She's excited about the topic, so she probably speaks more rapidly than the others.

• Willie is a little older and proud of his musical experience. His voice should communicate that pride. Ask students to model a few of his lines with a note of pride in their voices.

COMPREHENSION

After you read aloud the script, ask students these questions:

1. What instrument does Louis Armstrong want to play?

2. What does Louis mean when he says, "I want to be the man standing in the front!"

3. Willie is teasing Louis when he says, "I don't think I want to say!" How could you show that with your voice?

4. Do you think it was fair for the band leader to start Louis on the tambourine? Why or why not?

5. Do you think Willie's words helped Louis to accept playing the tambourine? Why or why not?

JAZZY AFTERNOON

PARTS

Narrator 1
Narrator 2
Narrator 3
Louis Armstrong: 12-year-old boy
Mr. Davis: school band director
Mrs. Johnson: school cook
Willie: 14-year-old boy
Stella: 12-year-old daughter of
   Mr. Davis

Narrator 1: It is late afternoon and a boy is sitting alone in a nearly empty room of a large, old house. The floors are hardwood, worn down by years of heavy use.

Narrator 2: The walls are covered in a faded wallpaper and there is a large chalkboard along one wall. All the windows are open. The air is warm and very humid.

Narrator 3: The year is 1912 and this is New Orleans. This is a reform school called the Colored Waif's Home for Boys. Conditions are an improvement over what many of the boys had at home.

Narrator 1: They learn trades such as carpentry and gardening. One of the greatest honors at the school is to be invited to join the band. This boy is one of the newest recruits.

Louis: I wanted to play the cornet.

Narrator 2: The cornet is similar to the trumpet, but it is smaller and slightly higher pitched.

Narrator 3: The school band director walks in. He has overheard the boy.

Mr. Davis: I know you do.

Louis: But you gave me a tambourine?

Mr. Davis: It will teach you to keep the beat and give you an opportunity to show me that I can trust you to work hard.

Louis: You can trust me!

Mr. Davis: Then it shouldn't be long before I can move you to a different instrument!

Narrator 1: There is a knock at the door. The school cook walks in with another boy.

Mrs. Johnson: Thanks for lending me your star pupil, Mr. Davis. He was a big help with lunch today!

Mr. Davis: Glad to hear it, Mrs. Johnson.

American History Reader's Theater © 2004 Creative Teaching Press

JAZZY AFTERNOON

Willie: Hi, Mr. Davis! You wanted to see me?

Mr. Davis: Willie, this is Louis Armstrong. He wants to be a cornet player someday.

Willie: How do you do?

Mr. Davis: Louis, this is Willie. He's our cornet player. We call him Tempo.

Louis: I have heard you play. You sound great!

Willie: Thanks! Everyone calls you Louis?

Louis: [laughing] Most folks do, but my friends back home call me Satchel Mouth.

Willie: I think I can see how you got that name. You have a big mouth when you smile!

Louis: And I like to smile. How did you get a name like Tempo?

Mrs. Johnson: He likes to tap out the beat with his head while he plays. Mr. Davis tried to get him to stop until he noticed it kept the rest of the band on the beat.

Mr. Davis: Willie, I want you to spend a few minutes with Louis here and show him how to use the tambourine for that piece we are performing Friday. Go get your instrument.

Willie: Sure thing, Mr. Davis.

Mrs. Johnson: I had better get things ready for supper. See you later, gentlemen.

Mr. Davis, Willie, and Louis: Bye, Mrs. Johnson.

Narrator 2: Willie leaves the room just as a girl enters.

Stella: Henry is on his way up, Papa.

Mr. Davis: Good, we need to leave soon to meet your mother. Louis, this is my daughter, Stella.

Narrator 3: Louis drops the tambourine.

Stella: Is that a tambourine?

Louis: Yes, sorry, I let it slip.

Stella: Is that what you get to play? You are so lucky!

Louis: The tambourine? Well, it's not a cornet . . .

Stella: Oh, I don't like the cornet. It makes your lips itch when they vibrate. But the tambourine is great. It can be like a drum, or make a soft noise like rain, or a loud noise like . . .

American History Reader's Theater © 2004 Creative Teaching Press

JAZZY AFTERNOON

Louis:	Locusts?
Stella:	Like a field of crickets!
Louis:	You must play it better than I can.
Stella:	Are you just learning? It's not hard. I think you are going to like it!
Narrator 1:	Willie reenters the room with his cornet.
Mr. Davis:	Stella, I will be waiting downstairs. Get your violin from the closet and meet me there.
Stella:	I will be right down, Papa! Nice meeting you . . .
Willie:	Satchel Mouth! We are calling him Satchel Mouth, Satch-a-mo, Satchmo, Satch!
Stella:	That's an odd name for a tambourine player!
Willie:	Satchmo is a tambourine player today, but he will be a cornet player someday, won't you, Louis?
Louis:	The best in the world!
Stella:	Well, I have to go, Satchel Mouth, but keep working on your tambourine and I am sure you will get your cornet.
Louis:	Nice meeting you, Stella.
Narrator 2:	Stella gets her violin from the closet and leaves to join her father. Louis sighs.
Willie:	He is really not doing it to punish you, Satch.
Louis:	I know, I do. It is an honor to be in the band and I am grateful for whatever instrument he hands me: tambourine, or rhythm sticks, or the triangle! But how many famous tambourine players do you know?
Willie:	I do not know many, but I do know a lot of famous bands where someone in the back plays the tambourine.
Louis:	See? I want to be the man standing in the front!
Willie:	How do you think the lead man got there? He just smiled real big and someone said, "Come on up! With teeth like that you have got to be our lead man!" We all have to start somewhere.

American History Reader's Theater © 2004 Creative Teaching Press

JAZZY AFTERNOON

Louis: You didn't start on the cornet?

Willie: Nope! When I first started, there was a boy named Henry on cornet. He finished his time and went home. That's when I got to move up. Mr. Davis only has one cornet, so only one kid at a time can play it.

Louis: What instrument did you start on?

Willie: I don't think I want to say!

Louis: Come on, it wasn't the tambourine was it?

Willie: No, it was a bell. I stood in the back next to the drums and played it for the Christmas songs we were doing that year.

Louis: How long did you play the bell?

Willie: Just a few weeks. Then I played the drums for six months and I have been on the cornet for the last year now.

Louis: I guess it could be good to play more than one instrument.

Willie: Let me get out my instrument and I will show you how this song goes. You want to sound good by Friday.

Louis: Who are we playing for?

Willie: An audience! I don't know exactly who. It does not matter as long as they like music.

Louis: Well, I like music!

Willie: Pick up your instrument then, Satchmo, and we will play some.

Narrator 3: Which is how Louis Armstrong, or Satchmo, one of the greatest of the New Orleans jazz musicians, began his formal music lessons.

American History Reader's Theater © 2004 Creative Teaching Press

RELATED LESSONS

Mardi Gras!

OBJECTIVE

Investigate the history of New Orleans through reading about Mardi Gras.

ACTIVITY

Explain that New Orleans was once a French colony and some modern traditions come from the French heritage. Read aloud a **book about Mardi Gras** such as *Mimi's First Mardi Gras* by Alice Couvillon (Pelican) or *Mardi Gras: A City's Masked Parade* by Lisa Gabbert (Powerkids). Provide students with some **online or print resources** to help them learn more about the festival or New Orleans history in general. Have students complete the **New Orleans! reproducible (page 78)** as they work.

ANSWERS

1. France
2. Spain
3. Fat Tuesday
4. The three official colors are purple, green, and gold. Purple represents justice. Green stands for faith. Gold stands for power.
5. Mardi Gras is celebrated on a Tuesday.
6. "Throw me some, Mister!"

Types of Jazz

ACTIVITY

Obtain from the library a **jazz collection on compact disc** that spans the genres of jazz such as big band, bop, cool, fusion, and New Orleans. One example of such a collection is *The Best of Ken Burns Jazz* (Sony)—which includes a classic Louis Armstrong recording. Before you play each piece, offer the information below about the genre. Play a sample of each genre, and then have students write a few reflective lines about the music. You may offer prompts such as *I like . . . , I do not like . . . ,* or *One thing I noticed about this piece was . . . .* Invite students to share some of their responses with the class.

New Orleans: The cornet or trumpet carries the melody, the clarinet plays a countermelody, and the trombone plays slides or longer low notes around the main melody. Drums and other bass instruments provide a rhythm. It was more important to play loudly and with great excitement than to play the notes perfectly.

Big Band: The biggest change was from a two-beat rhythm to a smoother four-beat rhythm. Musicians developed short patterns, called riffs, and played them back and forth, like a conversation, in the musical piece. An entire section of the orchestra would play one "voice" and another would "respond."

Bop: This genre features faster tempos, longer and more complex phrases, and a willingness to express unpleasant feelings through music. Earlier eras were more likely to explore pleasant emotions or express humor.

Cool: This music is soft in tone but highly complex.

Fusion Jazz: This genre features a mix of jazz sounds and styles with new technology and electronic instruments.

Name_____   Date _____

New Orleans!

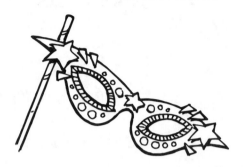

Directions: Use research materials about New Orleans and Mardi Gras to answer the following questions.

1. Which country first claimed New Orleans?

2. What other country owned New Orleans before it became part of the United States?

3. What does the name Mardi Gras mean in English?

4. What are the three official colors for Mardi Gras? What does each color represent?

5. On what day of the week is Mardi Gras celebrated?

6. What can you shout to earn beads, doubloons, and cups?

American History Reader's Theater © 2004 Creative Teaching Press

AMELIA
EARHART

AMERICAN
HISTORY

Vocabulary

Discuss each of the following words with students. Then, have students identify the word they least understand. Have students research this word and then draw an illustration that clarifies the definition.

albatross: a gangly seabird known for its lack of grace

flyer: an advertisement on a piece of paper and posted in public

plummets: drops steeply and suddenly downward

soars: rises high in the air

Background

A group of children visits the state fair. The sight of two planes inspires them to have a paper airplane race. Millie is Amelia Earhart. She really did see her first airplane at the state fair and she really was unimpressed with it. The paper hat is real. At that time in her life, she and her sister, Pidge, were living with their grandparents. The other characters are fictitious. However, Millie did train to be a nurse and, when she grew up, her flight instructor's first name was Anita. Finally, Anita's line at the top of page 84 about deciding whether the risks are worth it is a quote attributed to Earhart as an adult.

PARTS

Narrator 1
Narrator 2
Narrator 3
Millie: 10-year-old girl
Pidge: 8-year-old sister
Mr. Otis: grandfather to Millie and Pidge
Mrs. Otis: grandmother to Millie and Pidge
Kate: 9-year-old girl
Larry: 9-year-old friend
Tom: 10-year-old friend
Hank: 8-year-old friend
Anita: pilot

FLUENCY INSTRUCTION

Have students discuss the ages of the characters to help them reflect the maturity level in their reading. When you read aloud the script for students, have them listen for the following:

• The pace of the reading speeds up when children are excited. Have students name at least three places where the reading pace will pick up in this script.

• Mr. and Mrs. Otis are grandparents to Millie and Pidge. Ask students how they can show with their voices that these characters are older adults.

• Your voice rises at the end of a question, such as in the line *Larry:* *What do you know about airplanes?*

COMPREHENSION

After you read aloud the script, ask students these questions:

1. Who are Millie and Pidge?

2. How do Millie and Pidge seem different from each other?

3. Find two places in the story where your voice would rise for a question.

4. What was the reason Millie decided to participate in the race?

5. Do you think Millie's first sight of an airplane influenced her decision to eventually learn to fly? Why or why not?

MILLIE AND THE PAPER AIRPLANE

PARTS

Narrator 1
Narrator 2
Narrator 3
Millie: 10-year-old girl
Pidge: 8-year-old sister
Mr. Otis: grandfather to Millie
   and Pidge
Mrs. Otis: grandmother to Millie
   and Pidge
Kate: 9-year-old girl
Larry: 9-year-old friend
Tom: 10-year-old friend
Hank: 8-year-old friend
Anita: pilot

Narrator 1: It is mid-day on a fine spring day in Iowa. The year is 1907 and it is the state fair.

Narrator 2: A young girl and her sister are attending the fair with their grandparents and a large group of friends.

Narrator 3: They are walking past the exhibits, having just finished a picnic lunch prepared by the girls' grandmother.

Millie: Oh my, look at that!

Mr. Otis: Put away your pennies, Millie. You do not need those sweets. Your grandmother has a pie waiting for us at home.

Mrs. Otis: Strawberry!

Pidge and Larry: Mmmmm, my favorite!

Tom: Ooh, Mrs. Otis, maybe you will need help with a pie like that?

Millie: Never mind the pie, look at those lovely hats!

Pidge: That pink one is rather pretty.

Millie: It's not pink, Pidge. It's peach. There is a difference.

Hank: You never wear hats, Millie! I swear if you had the chance you would wear trousers!

Mrs. Otis: A tendency to climb trees does not mean she cannot wear appropriate dress. I think that hat would look wonderful on you, my dear.

Mr. Otis: [grumbling] It is not a wonderful price though.

Mrs. Otis: We will think about it and perhaps come back for it. That is rather a lot of money for a paper hat.

MILLIE AND THE PAPER AIRPLANE

Kate: Stop thinking about hats and look at that man and woman!

Mr. Otis: Judging by the way they are dressed, those two are pilots.

Pidge: Pilots?

Millie: You know, airplane pilots. Maybe we could see their planes!

Mr. Otis: We could follow them . . .

Tom and Larry: Let's go!

Kate: Oh! Wait! I think I see the planes!

Millie: Where?

Tom: She means those things.

Millie: Those old pieces of rusty wire and wood? They look like large, old barrels!

Hank: Kind of disappointing really.

[The group is quiet.]

Tom: I know an airplane that will fly high, high through the sky!

Larry: What do you know about airplanes?

Tom: I know enough to make my own!

Kate: Quit bragging and show us then.

Mr. Otis: [laughing] I think I know your sort of plane. Let me help you with the materials.

Narrator 1: Mr. Otis walks to the nearest food stand. A flyer advertising the fair is stuck to its side.

Narrator 2: Mr. Otis carefully peels the flyer off the stand, so as not to tear it.

Mr. Otis: Here you go, son.

Tom: Perfect, Mr. Otis, sir! Thank you!

Narrator 3: Tom starts carefully turning, folding, and pressing the creases of the paper. He holds his finished creation high.

Tom: I call her the Kittyhawk!

Millie: Oh, clever name, Tom!

American History Reader's Theater © 2004 Creative Teaching Press

MILLIE AND THE PAPER AIRPLANE

Kate: I do not know how clever the plane is though.

Larry: Let's see it fly!

Narrator 1: Tom pulls his arm back and pushes the plane swiftly into the sky.

Narrator 2: It soars high, floats for a bit . . .

Narrator 3: . . . then plummets to the ground.

Hank: Not bad! Show me how to make one!

Millie: Oh! Me, too!

Pidge: I see another flyer!

Narrator 1: Each child runs off to get a flyer. Mr. Otis and Tom show the others how to fold the paper to make an airplane.

Millie: Mine is the, um, the Sunrise.

Pidge: Oh, will we each name our plane? Mine is the Albatross then.

Larry: [laughing] Oh, that's a graceful bird! Mine is the Eagle. Very noble.

Kate: I do not have a clever name for my plane, but I will bet it is faster than your sunrises, albatrosses, and eagles!

Tom: Oh, a bet then! Yes! Let us have a race!

Mr. Otis: All right then, I am feeling generous. Winner gets a treat of his or her choice.

Mrs. Otis: I will judge.

Hank: No, wait! Here come the pilots! Let's see if they will judge for us!

Narrator 2: The group waves the pilots over to them.

Larry: We are having a contest to see which plane can fly the furthest distance!

Anita: The furthest! What about which can do the most loops?! The greatest dive?

Kate: Oh, that will be Tom's plane then!

Millie: I don't know about this . . . seems kind of a silly thing to race a paper airplane!

Tom: Since when were you one to back down from a challenge?

Millie: I didn't say I was backing down! I just said it seemed kind of silly!

MILLIE AND THE PAPER AIRPLANE

Anita: Decide whether or not the goal is worth the risks involved. If it is, quit worrying.

Millie: I do want that peach paper hat!

Mrs. Otis: Then you had better fly that plane as far as she will go!

Anita: All right then! Here is the starting line.

Narrator 3: The kids line up with their airplanes.

Anita: On your mark, get set, FLY!

Narrators: The paper planes are pushed into the sky.

Narrator 1: Kate's plane flies straight up, falters, twists to the side, and plummets back to her feet.

Narrator 2: Tom's plane flies straight out for 7 feet, tilts to the left, and glides gracefully sideways to the ground. His plane travels a total of 9 feet from the starting line.

Narrator 3: Pidge's plane flies out a few feet, does a spectacular loop, and then travels quickly to the ground for a total of 7 feet.

Narrator 1: Larry's plane flies up and out for 10 feet, but then suddenly it twists and flies back 7 feet to land 3 feet from where it started.

Narrator 2: Millie's plane flies straight out, slowly, wobbly, but it floats gently along until it comes to rest 15 feet from the starting line.

All Kids: Yay, Millie! You did it! Nice going!

Mr. Otis: I guess I owe you a hat then!

Anita: Nice flying, kids! Good job, little Millie. Maybe when you are older, I will see you in a proper airplane!

Mrs. Otis: Oh my, that sounds dangerous!

Millie: Oh, Grandma, you worry too much! Besides, I do not think I want to be a pilot. I want to be a nurse or a doctor!

Anita: [laughing] We will see, Millie. I guess we will just have to wait and see.

American History Reader's Theater © 2004 Creative Teaching Press

RELATED LESSONS

Experimenting with Flight

OBJECTIVE
Research information about Amelia Earhart and write a poem about her.

ACTIVITY

Provide students with **books about Amelia Earhart.** Divide the class into small groups, and have them use the books to learn more about the pilot. Then, give each student a **Bio Poem reproducible (page 86)** to write about her. Have students share their completed poem with the class.

Will It Fly?

OBJECTIVE
Research types of flying machines throughout history.

ACTIVITY

Provide students with **online and print resources** with pictures and information about a variety of flying machines (real and imagined) throughout history. If time is limited, encourage students to work in small groups. Have students draw the machine of their choice in the box on the **Will It Fly? reproducible (page 87)** and tell about it in a short paragraph. Bind the completed reproducibles into a class book.

Name_____ Date _____

Bio Poem

Directions: Before you begin, read about Amelia Earhart. Then, follow the directions below each line to write a poem about her.

_____

(First name)

_____

(Her job or occupation)

_____

(Four adjectives that describe her)

Sister of _____

(Name of her sister and/or brother)

Lover of _____

(3 or more things or ideas)

Who believes _____

(1 or more ideas)

Who wants _____

(3 or more things or ideas)

Who says _____

(a quote)

_____

(Last name)

American History Reader's Theater © 2004 Creative Teaching Press

Name_____ Date _____

Will It Fly?

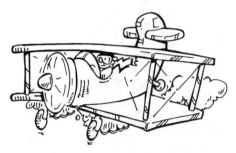

Directions: Draw your flying machine in the large box. Then write a paragraph that describes it below.

[large blank box]

_____

_____

_____

_____

_____

_____

American History Reader's Theater © 2004 Creative Teaching Press

THE ERA OF THE MODEL T

AMERICAN HISTORY

VOCABULARY

Discuss each of the following words with students. Then, have students choose one of the words to research in a print or online dictionary. Have students create a chart that teaches the class more about that word.

clutch: a part of a car that allows the car to move from one gear to another

loaves: plural of "loaf"

patient: capable of waiting

satisfied: happy and content

scurry: run back and forth

startled: jumped from surprise

BACKGROUND

A farm family takes their first ride in a brand-new Model T car. Although it seems that a farmer might have purchased a tractor before a car, the invention of the tractor did not immediately follow the invention of the car and they were not affordable for the average farmer at this time. The Model T was difficult to start, using a crank set at the front of the vehicle. It was not unheard of for the kick of the engine to cause the crank to spin around and break the arm of the person turning it. Unpaved roads with deep ruts made for very bumpy rides. Going for a drive with the family was a social event. The title comes from a quote attributed to Henry Ford. He is believed to have joked that "you can paint it any color, so long as it's black."

PARTS

↑ Narrator 1
↑ Narrator 2
  Mr. Jones: Alabama farmer
  Mrs. Jones: Alabama farm wife
  Stephanie: 12-year-old girl
↓ Rebecca: 10-year-old girl
  Matthew: 8-year-old boy
↓ Abby: 5-year-old girl
  Max: 6-year-old boy

FLUENCY INSTRUCTION

Have students discuss the ages of the characters to help them reflect the maturity level in their reading. When you read aloud the script for students, have them listen for the following:

• The pitch and volume both increase slightly when the father yells to the preacher.

• Some of these characters are quite young. Have students model a variety of ways to sound younger.

• Your volume increases substantially when you are surprised. Have students find a place in the script when the family is very surprised.

COMPREHENSION

After you read aloud the script, ask students these questions:

1. How does Mr. Jones have to start the car?

2. How would you describe the family's new car?

3. How would you choose to show Mrs. Jones' excitement at the beginning of the story?

4. Why do you think Mr. Jones forgot to put in the clutch towards the end of the story when he stopped the car?

5. Do you think Mr. Jones eventually bought that tractor? Why or why not?

YOU CAN PAINT IT ANY COLOR

PARTS

Narrator 1
Narrator 2
Mr. Jones: Alabama farmer
Mrs. Jones: Alabama farm wife
Stephanie: 12-year-old girl
Rebecca: 10-year-old girl
Matthew: 8-year-old boy
Abby: 5-year-old girl
Max: 6-year-old boy

Narrator 1: A small child comes running in the back door of a modest family home in Georgia.

Matthew: Mama, Mama, he did it! Daddy bought a Model T!

Mrs. Jones: Did you see him coming this way?

Matthew: He is driving across the field, coming up from the Coopers' place!

Narrator 2: More feet are heard pounding up the steps through the back door and into the kitchen.

Rebecca: You can hear it! It sounds just like Mr. Cooper's Model T!

Abby: It looks just like it, too!

Max: But it is new!

Stephanie: Oh, Mama, can we all go for a ride?

Narrator 1: Mrs. Jones places two loaves of bread to rise on the counter. She eyes the bread and looks over the kitchen.

Narrator 2: It is clean and neat and she is satisfied.

Mrs. Jones: Let us go see our new family car! Of course, we must take it for a ride! Hats and coats! Shoes and socks!

Narrator 1: The Jones children scurry around the house looking for clothes to go out in.

Narrator 2: They are about to go for their first drive.

Narrator 1: Chugging noisily, the car pulls to a stop in front of the house.

Mr. Jones: What do you think, Mother?

Mrs. Jones: It is rather handsome, don't you think? Will we all fit?

Mr. Jones: Oh, we will find a way! Climb in, kids!

American History Reader's Theater © 2004 Creative Teaching Press

YOU CAN PAINT IT ANY COLOR

Mrs. Jones: You can sit up front with me, Max. Stephanie, you hold Abby on your lap.

Matthew: I want to sit on the outside!

Mr. Jones: I want you in the middle between your big sisters. Now everyone be patient. It seems to be a bit of a trick to get her started.

Narrator 2: Mr. Jones walks to the front of the car. A long metal handle sticks out from the front of the grill.

Narrator 1: He grabs the crank and turns it once quickly. The engine catches, then dies. He turns it again quickly. This time the engine catches and then chugs to life.

Narrator 2: This is a new car, and Mr. Jones does not have a lot of driving experience. He lets the clutch out too fast and the car lurches forward . . .

All: Whoah!

Narrator 2: . . . and dies.

Narrator 1: He climbs out, restarts the car, climbs back in, and this time gently eases out the clutch as he puts the car in gear.

Narrator 2: With a medium-sized lurch, the car moves forward.

Max: We are off!

Mrs. Jones: Is it always that hard to start?

Mr. Jones: Oh, I imagine I just need to get used to it.

Mrs. Jones: Thank goodness there are no hills around here!

Mr. Jones: I was thinking the same thing on the ride home!

Mrs. Jones: Will we go back across the field?

Mr. Jones: It is too bumpy for this crowd. I am afraid our family would be smaller by the end of it. We will head down the carriage path at the front of the house and out to the road.

Rebecca: We can go get gas at the new service station by the general store!

Mr. Jones: I do not believe we have gone far enough to use up any gas, dear. I was thinking we would drive over to Blackberry Pond and back.

American History Reader's Theater © 2004 Creative Teaching Press

You Can Paint It Any Color

Stephanie: Oh, it is beautiful over there this time of year.

Matthew: Did we bring any bread to feed the ducks?

Mrs. Jones: I think I have some here in my pocket.

Max: Blow the horn! Blow the horn!

Stephanie: Oh, there is the preacher and his wife! Yes, blow the horn so they see us and wave!

Mrs. Jones: Don't make a scene, dear.

Narrator 1: But Mr. Jones gleefully blows the horn three times. It is very loud and the children are startled and cover their ears.

Matthew: Oh, that is too loud!

Max: It was OK. Do it again!

Stephanie and Rebecca: No! No, that is enough.

Narrator 2: The preacher and his wife wave back at the passing family.

Mrs. Jones: It is so bumpy here! Try to stay to the right of the ruts.

Mr. Jones: I am trying, but the ruts are so deep that once I am in, I cannot get out!

Mrs. Jones: Up there by the tree, there is a flat spot.

Mr. Jones: I see it.

Narrator 2: As Mr. Jones gets to a spot in the road where the ruts flatten out into a smoother road, he steers to the right to try to avoid the deep spaces left by wagon wheels when the road was muddy.

Narrator 1: He goes too far though, and the right wheel is off the road and onto the grass.

Stephanie: Too bumpy! Too bumpy! Slow down or I will fall out!

Narrator 2: Mr. Jones panics and slams on the brakes.

Narrator 1: He forgets to put in the clutch. There is another large lurch forward and the car dies.

All: Aaah!

Mr. Jones: Oh my, I hope this gets easier!

American History Reader's Theater © 2004 Creative Teaching Press

YOU CAN PAINT IT ANY COLOR

Mrs. Jones: You had better get used to it. You saw that tractor at the state fair this year! They say that is the future!

Mr. Jones: I think I have some time to practice. Our farm will not be getting a tractor anytime soon. Still, we can't have the children falling out because I cannot drive the thing.

Matthew: You are doing great, Dad!

Stephanie: Can I drive?

Abby: If she drives, I am walking.

Max: If she drives, I want to drive!

Mrs. Jones: No one but your father is starting this machine. Settle down.

Narrator 2: Mr. Jones turns the crank, but it only makes a single low RAR that dies quickly.

Narrator 1: He turns it again. RAR.

Narrator 2: This is hard work. He starts to sweat. He turns it twice more, rapidly. RAR. RAR.

Mrs. Jones: Don't fidget children. He will get it started.

Mr. Jones: I don't know. It didn't make this noise before.

Mrs. Jones: Everyone out. We will let the car rest a moment and then try again. You can feed the ducks.

Narrator 1: The children chase the ducks. After a few minutes, Mr. Jones, now in despair and thinking of all the money he spent on his new car, tries with a heavy heart to start the car again.

Narrator 2: It roars to life and spits and sputters.

Mr. Jones: There it is! Everyone in! I think that is enough of a drive for today!

Matthew: Nice going, Dad!

Narrator 1: The preacher and his wife pass in their horse and carriage.

Narrator 2: The preacher calls out a compliment to the car and the family in it.

Mr. Jones: Thank you, Reverend! I think highly of them both!

American History Reader's Theater © 2004 Creative Teaching Press

RELATED LESSON

Cart Versus Horse

OBJECTIVE

Research the advantages and disadvantages of the horse and cart and the car. Argue the benefits of one and the disadvantages of each.

ACTIVITY

Explain briefly that a debate is a contest where two sides present information in favor of a particular position. The side that offers better information is considered the winner. Tell students that you will host a debate to discuss which is a better method of transportation: the horse and cart or the car. Point out that both methods of transportation are still in use in the world, even here in the United States where some groups such as the Amish choose to use one over the other. Tell students that you will start them off with a couple of debate points and they will research horses, carts, and cars to add to those points. Then, they will pair up in a debate. Divide the class into small groups of three to five students. Give each group a card from the **Cart and Car reproducible (page 95)** and access to **print or online research materials** such as encyclopedias or children's magazine articles. Point out that the card has room for points for and against each side to be made and rebuttal arguments. Explain that in a debate you respond to a point that the other team made about why their vehicle is good with a rebuttal that shows why that argument is weak or incorrect but the rebuttal must be true. On the card, the information used in *against* may be used as part of the rebuttal. Explain that every point will not have a rebuttal. You can also assign the research as a homework assignment to encourage parent involvement. Then, pair teams to host the debate. You may want to present the first debate with another adult, or put on different hats to show yourself arguing first for the horse and cart and then for the car. As an option, use the **Debate Scoring Rubric (page 96)** to score the debates. This activity can be paired with an activity that teaches students how to write a bibliography for their source materials.

Cart and Car

For the Horse and Cart

1. A horse does not make air or noise pollution.

2.

3.

4.

Against the Car

1. A car makes a lot more noise than a horse. It disturbs the neighborhood when you drive it at night.

2.

3.

4.

For the Car

1. A car never gets tired.

2.

3.

4.

Against the Horse and Cart

1. A horse can get sick and die suddenly. You cannot buy a simple part to fix it. You have to get a whole new horse.

2.

3.

4.

Debate Scoring Rubric

Directions: If you use a rubric to score the debates, be sure to discuss each area with students ahead of time so they are clear about your expectations. You might use just one of these areas or all three.

Arguments

4—Superior: Arguments were eloquent, complex, elaborated, and supported with evidence and examples.

3—Proficient: Arguments were complex, elaborated, and supported with evidence and examples.

2—Essential: Arguments were supported with evidence and examples.

1—Unsatisfactory: Arguments lacked evidence and support.

Rebuttal

4—Superior: Rebuttal directly addressed each of the opponents' arguments with counterevidence.

3—Proficient: Rebuttal directly addressed most of the opponents' arguments with counterevidence.

2—Essential: Rebuttal directly addressed some of the opponents' arguments with counterevidence.

1—Unsatisfactory: Rebuttal did not directly address the opponents' arguments and/or did not present counterevidence.

Teamwork

4—Superior: Each member of the team presented an argument that built on the arguments of those that came earlier.

3—Proficient: Each member of the team presented different but complementary arguments.

2—Essential: Each member of the team presented a different argument, with minimal overlap and repetition.

1—Unsatisfactory: Arguments were overlapping, repetitive, or contradictory.

American History Reader's Theater © 2004 Creative Teaching Press